D1395403

Language of My Choosing

Language of My Choosing
The candid life-memoir of an Italian Scot

ANNE PIA

Luath Press Limited

EDINBURGH

www.luath.co.uk

First published 2017

ISBN: 978-1910745-91-5

The author's right to be identified as author of this book
under the Copyright, Designs and Patents Act 1988 has been asserted.

The paper used in this book is recyclable. It is made
from low chlorine pulps produced in a low energy,
low emission manner from renewable forests.

Printed and bound by ScandBook AB, Sweden

Typeset in 11 point Sabon

Camilla, Roberta, Sophie-Louise, I dedicate this book to you. With all my love.

Contents

Acknowledgments

Without the help and support of the following, this book would never have been written: Geraldine Doherty, Sheila McMillan, Monica Gibb, Fiona Durkin, Dr Carlo Pirozzi, University of Edinburgh; and Alan Gay.

I would also like to thank Linda Menzies, Nina Craighead and Marion Newbery for reading and providing comments on first drafts and my patient editors, Hilary Bell and Jennie Renton at Luath Press. Grateful thanks are also due to Eastern Western Motor Group, Edinburgh.

Thank you lastly, to Paul and our three daughters, Camilla, Roberta, Sophie-Louise for their support, realism and love.

Author's Note

THIS BOOK EVOKES a period in time. It is a first-hand account of life in one immigrant family and a portrayal of the changing Scottish Italian community in Edinburgh over a forty-year span. Together with English, the rich dialect of Viticuso, which I spoke with my grandmother, was a mother tongue and I have offered some insights into the relationship of Italian Scots with that language. I hope that I have both paid tribute to that raw language of intimacy and humour and encouraged others to own and be proud of that fine legacy.

As I write, universal concerns about immigration and the movement of people dominate world politics. I explain from my experience of racism after World War Two, that integration is often painful and challenging with regard to family and social relationships; and how the exclusion of one group by another dominating culture can breed a potentially dangerous counter offensive. It leaves many of us affected by it, dislocated, damaged and disoriented.

This is my story about finding my identity through my gradual distancing from the background of loss and alienation that I grew up in. It is a tale of strength, self-belief and optimism.

Anne Pia

Openings

A Complicated Relationship with Milk

I HAVE ALWAYS had a complicated relationship with milk. My ways with it are erratic. There are the obvious connections linking it with maternity and nurturing of course. You may know of the intriguing mythology surrounding the pagan goddess Brigit of Kildare. Her popularity to this day in Ireland almost equals that of Mary. Brigit was the Sun Goddess, a warrior maiden, a symbol of sexual purity, and came to be associated with the milk of cows, the sacred food of the Celts. So great was her popularity that she was finally imported into the Christian canon. She has become a symbol of the transition from paganism to Christianity. However, my revulsion at milk, which is neither consistent nor universal, has no underlying meaning; there is nothing to be read into it since I had no difficulty whatsoever with motherhood or indeed with Brigit or those issues which I see as choice, for sexuality and purity are elective. Nor has it anything to do with taste; no, my lack of predictability with milk, the ability to drink it with coffee but never on its own and absolutely never in tea, goes back to my childhood.

From Bruntsfield Links to my convent primary school in Edinburgh was a ten-minute walk. It was my most anxious time of the day, except maybe when my mother herself was anxious, uneasy or distracted, which was really always. That is how I remember the mother of my childhood. And so, like her, I spent my days with a low level feeling of disquiet which I at least knew had nothing to do with me, but which was heightened first thing in the morning.

I also knew not to be obvious. There were more important things going on which I was not to interrupt. My nights, when darkest thoughts are made material and when we can pinpoint exactly what we are most afraid of, were easier than daytime. At night, I was able to surface. The fear of balconies crashing to the ground in a theatre, of being bombed by jets overhead or of the sea engulfing and choking me, those things came later.

My earliest memories are of life in our second storey flat in Morningside opposite the Plaza dance hall, where we – my mother, father and I – lived with my grandmother. It was her house and she always told us so. There were two double beds in my mother's bedroom and I shared one of them with my mother. I felt no anxiety at night, except maybe occasionally at the unexplained empty bed across the room.

My first day at school was in September 1954. On that first morning, I was led through the dark oak-panelled corridor of a Victorian house. There was a stairway that curved all the way up to a window and another floor, a long mirror at one end and a glass-panelled door leading to the front garden at the other. I can never remember that door being open. We generally came in at the back, through the playground, where the cloakrooms were and the little window where at break time the nuns sold tablet, a Scottish sugary favourite best eaten, in my view, when it had failed and was soft and sticky.

A nun, my teacher for the year, all in black, her tight small features made even less appealing by the stiff white surround of her wimple, and whose tone was more suited to litany than light conversation, took me to my desk in the second row of a room full of children of my age. I was given a slate and chalk to write on; there was an inkwell; the desks were attached to the wooden seats and so the positioning was fixed. We went to the classroom door to say goodbye to my mother and she pointed to a throne-like seat outside the room, saying she would wait for me there until the break. I saw crates of small bottles of milk beside the throne. When break came, I ran to the door to check if she was still there. She wasn't. I was lost, maybe in some ways lost well into my adult life, and certainly to milk.

From then on, every morning as we crossed the links, me in my not one but *two* pairs of knickers, one white and one navy with a pocket, lumpy in navy gabardine stretched tight over my blazer, laced brogues to correct flat feet, I cried, retched and vomited all the way to Whitehouse Loan, my mother hurrying me along. I could do nothing to stop it and it was important, I knew, not to hold my mother up but to keep going.

When the milk crate was brought into the classroom at break and placed at the French doors to the convent garden, I had to struggle not to bring attention to myself by being sick in front of my classmates. Along with the nausea at the sight and smell of the milk, was the cracked green crust under the nose of the girl next to me; the sight of the slipper, used only on the worst-behaved boys; the daily use of the ruler; and the confusing practice the teacher had of choosing someone to sit on her knee for some time during the afternoon lesson. I guessed this signalled good temper and a trouble-free rest of the day.

A woman who witnessed the spectacle of our halting pathway across the grass every day, once said to my mother 'I don't know how you have the heart to take her to school.' On a few occasions I did make an effort with breakfast, usually porridge, but it came back up soon enough and so I stopped having breakfast completely. That morning feeling of faint nausea, together with an anxiety that might arise at any time, sometimes for no reason, have accompanied me for much of my life and only in more recent years have early-morning avocado, eggs, toasted artisan bread and crushed tomatoes with olive oil become a real pleasure.

In writing this book, I have been inspired by Elena Ferrante. In her Neapolitan novels, she writes about the lives of people living in a suburb of Naples and their struggle to make something of their lives... there were those who stayed and those who left... those who returned and those who stayed away, never quite able to shake off their origins. What they had come from continued to threaten to repossess them at every crossroads, at every high and especially at every low, at each failure and success in their lives.

I don't know what it was that made life in my Italian home in Edinburgh in the post-war years so raw, so relentless, merciless and destructive, so deadening to the spirit, to love and joy. It seemed that every area of one's life was a family affair to be considered, approved or not; intrusive, judgemental and directive. The power in my home resided in the matriarch, my grandmother, and her son, Enrico (Rico), both of whom monitored, allocated, punished, and schemed. My mother was a servant to their plans... a pawn really, her life nothing but a strand of family business, her marriage partly destroyed by them and partly by her own bid for freedom from the family system. Yet my mother herself (maybe with age came regression), sought to reel me back in to what she herself had desperately tried to escape.

The memories of those dark early years are of frustration at my powerlessness; of indignation at my mother's subservience, head down, bending to the will of her brother, chastised for not; a childhood of fear; of physical violence; of a grandmother wary and cunning, rosary in hand, candles in her bedroom, who both loved and cursed; and who beat her head on the wall to bring about angina attacks when thwarted. She was a woman of great physical strength who could throw Ernestina, an Italian cousin who came to help in the house, to the ground and upturn an entire set table minutes before Christmas lunch. Rico was an uncle who slapped his sister, my mother, then wept. He was violent to his son to the point where police were called to our house in Bruntsfield. He and my grandmother were suspicious, always watchful of my mother because of her glamour, her makeup and free spirit... *na puttan,* slut, were words I knew well.

I saw it all, and I wanted to leave it all behind... the system, the family, the values, the insidious control of spirit and aspiration; the robbing of us, the new generation, of what it was to be young and hopeful... to be happy. There was no happiness there in that tragedy. I remember no laughter around my grandmother, only secrecy, subterfuge, pulsating resentments.

Chi pecore se fa, gle lup' se la magne, act the sheep and the wolf will eat you. So I did leave it behind through my education, an advantage my mother struggled hard against that system to give me, and my own ability and skill not only to thrive at school, at university, but to seek and know those who could inspire me, give me the gifts of culture, music, and poetry. And I connected, clung to and learned from them, and in their company I lived and breathed, was able to move away. In their orbit I embraced and developed with them, values very different from where I had come. I held these values close, silently, and I rarely challenged the family structure. I just determinedly moved away with each step I took and throughout my life, even into my sixties, I have lived those values and dropped almost every family connection: the lifestyle, mindsets and values which my southern Italian family and the Italian community stood for.

My marriage was to be I thought, a definitive final ascent from that ghetto; a positive move, together with my husband, to create something of ours; our joint desire to leave the family, the system, and create our own professional, liberal lifestyle of equality, refinement, culture and the arts. I had a vision of a professional couple sharing, growing and learning every day; with each new baby and each new career move, gaining distance from where we had been; putting that repressive, gut-wrenching old order based on survival in different times and a different context – the village, the war – behind us. Indeed I saw us criticising, challenging and despising what it had tried to do to each of us. And I saw an intelligent, artistic lifestyle, a family thriving within it, a life of gentle art and ideas, of idealism and creativity. I also know that increasingly in my years after school when I chose an honours degree, a career in secondary, rather than primary teaching, which my uncle tried to persuade me into; when I went to live in France, got married, got pregnant; had one, two and then a third child; when I left the classroom, went to work in Glasgow; made career moves which involved daily commuting to places other than Edinburgh; when I began to argue for the ordinary people, assert women's rights – I know that I became someone my mother no longer recognised. While she was always proud of me, she didn't know me... could not reckon with me. She would look at me in a puzzled way. It was as if she had never taken account of the energy and vision that I had been covertly nurturing all my childhood years. Here I was, hers, and yet very much not hers.

What Ferrante brings out in her books about Naples, is that whether you stay within the system, the ghetto, or leave, grow, become a respected and successful professional, the ghetto never quite leaves you; and those who were there with you, those who travel away from it with you, will always treat you as if you are still both in the potato fields of your origins, the stables you shared with your animals. The same rough, disrespectful language; the same roles and the same pecking order. A doctorate you may have, a respected role in society you may hold, but in that vice of the old ways, of *gl' Vtratur*, and those of *gl' Piciniscar* (the languages and ways of Viticuso and Picinisco) you are as you were.

In order to hold on to where I have reached, the life I have made, in order to maintain my construct of self, hewn out of distress and insecurity and the omnipresent light of the goal I seek, I have to keep that distance. And in doing that I am always conflicted. Increasingly as years pass, I yearn for home, the home of familiar, of ordinary, of history, of my dialect, of the customs I knew and the syntax and cadencing of those who went before me. But I know and fear that in embracing them, in that homecoming, I will sacrifice a life's work and deny all I saw and hoped for at the outset; and I know too that for those who stayed, and for those who came even a little way with me, who left only for a little while, I will always be nothing but a woman they think they know, rather than the conflicted achiever, the constant pilgrim that I am.

Wolfgang Tillmans, Turner prizewinner and German cult artist, whose work I discovered very recently, describes his work as a series of constellations of pictures, a way of seeing the world, not in a linear order but as a multitude of parallel experiences. I have taken a similar approach in this book. It is not a chronological account of my life. There are many aspects which I have not included; some questions are left unanswered. In each of the chapters I have tried to represent that ongoing dialogue between the experiences of my past, my present and who I choose and want to be; to indicate the competing forces that have led to certainty and doubt in my journey; and to offer insights into the influences of these on my self-making and self-actualisation, leading to who I am now.

Every experience is continually present in my life. Certain of these life events and people have been significant in taking me forward. In this account, backlighting those key influences and influencers, like players on a stage awaiting their cue, indicates their significance and their role; highlights and more specifically spotlights, bring increasing focus. Footlights signal an ending.

Backlights – Backdrop to My Life

Where it All Started: Viticuso, Lazio, Italy

MY STORY STARTS in a place I have never lived in, a place I have visited as a tourist only. Viticuso, the home of my grandparents. This visiting of Viticuso, in the Province of Frosinone, and Italy more generally, has always been a disconcerting experience... knowing at a glance the spirit and instincts of people you meet, the familiarity of a mannerism, a look, a jawline, an emotional stirring, the strongest urge to reach out as if to your own, tear at barriers that upbringing, history and geography have created.

Viticuso and the Lazio region of Italy were badly affected during World War Two. The monument Mamma Ciociara, reaching out from the Rocca di San Pietro in La Ciociaría in Central Italy, is the region's tribute to the thousands of women aged eleven to eighty-six who were dragged by the hair like livestock, beaten and then raped by Les Goumiers, Moroccan auxiliaries in the French army. It is also a memorial to the eight hundred men shot, stabbed and cut down as they tried to defend their children, wives, daughters, mothers and sisters. Though in fact, when there was a choice and despite the pleas of mothers to offer themselves and spare their children, the preference was always for the youngest of the families.

Accounts of that May night in 1944, the night of the Allies' victory at Montecassino, describe animal screaming across the Lazio area, as village after village came under the control not of Americans bearing candy for the children, which was what they expected, but of Moroccan troops as they swarmed across the countryside, leaving bloodied devastation behind them.

Silvio Palombo, a local resident, described the experience:

Portavano delle tuniche, così, di tutti i colori. portavano dei capelli lunghi, sporchi, in un modo che non sembravano nemmeno truppe, sembravano gente raccattata. Noi stavamo aspettando gli americani, la cioccolata. Quelle grida che ho sentito io quella notte, erano un'inferno, un inferno dantesco. Sembravano quelle belve che sbranavano gli animali... quella notte fu terribile.

They wore tunics, of all colours, had long hair. They were filthy and didn't look like troops at all. They were like jail breakers, criminals. We were expecting the Americans, chocolate... those screams that I heard that night... it was like hell... a scene from Dante's inferno. The sounds were like animals howling... it was a terrible night.

Often women were taken by two soldiers, sodomised and raped at the same time. Many women died as a result of those attacks.

The monument in Castro dei Volsci, where seven thousand civilians, including children were raped, is both sensual and ethereal; is like a spirit rising untouched from the battered bodies of these brave women: Mamma Ciociara in continual flight across the hillsides of that proud land, her womanhood ever and only hers.

Viticuso was one of those villages. It had originally been founded in medieval times by the monks of Montecassino to provide the abbey with supplies. Montecassino itself was a key stronghold, eight hundred metres above sea level on the Gustav Line separating Nazi and Fascist Italy from the Allied advance from the south. The outcome of the 1944 battle would determine the outcome of the war.

It was this village, Viticuso, which produced Paolozzi, Cocozza and Mario Lanza, my relations, the artists, singers and musicians, so heralded and honoured in the post-war era. It was this village, so uniquely bound up with the fate of Montecassino, which my grandparents left for Edinburgh in Scotland, in the belief that, as in America, the streets were 'paved with gold'.

I have only become aware of what it was like to live these events in Italy late in life. I had known the story of those who left Italy, the struggle of my own family settled in Edinburgh since 1913 and those like them, Italians across Scotland, after Italy entered the war. I found the accounts by chance, have been shaken by them. But later came the slow realisation of what it had been like not only for those Italians, my mother, grandmother and grandfather, treated as enemy aliens, but also for those relations who stayed behind: the imposition of German soldiers on their homes and frugal supplies, the daily shelling and bombardment of Montecassino, gunfire, aircraft, bombs, grenades, soldiers on motorbikes, soldiers on the hills, soldiers marching. The rubble that Cassino itself became, and the *Marocchinate* as those violent events, principally against women and children, came to be called.

Reading about that history, and hearing interviews with those who remembered, brought to mind from years back a photograph in a Sunday newspaper: a deserted expanse of land, dust, stones and plaster; in the centre of the photo, a man and a little boy walking hand in hand along what had once been the main street in Cassino.

The Night Neighbours Became the Enemy

MUSSOLINI DECLARED WAR on Britain and France on 10 June 1940. My mother, Cristina Rossi was 'minding' the family café in Edinburgh's Leith Walk on her own that night. The family had made its pilgrim way from the Bonnington area; from selling ice cream from a barrel, from living in the back shop, to setting solid foot on Victorian Leith Walk. For immigrants, 'arriving' was to be located in Edinburgh. The nearer to that border between Leith and Edinburgh, the more successful a family saw itself to be. So, in the good Italian traditions of *bella figura*... how we present in the world, the orange boxes in the back of the Bonnington shop were replaced by beds for the children in a flat above Shrubhill Café. My grandmother Maria, Mariuccia, Mary, Mrs Rossi, indeed, 'The Duchess', took to wearing satin overalls behind her shop counter and white gloves for shopping trips to Darlings of Edinburgh or a trip to Peebles in a taxi for a two week break at the Hydro. She had acquired the manner and dress of a lady. She wore them with dignity.

Business, even for a summer's evening, was slow and my mother, aged twenty-three, was staring out of the shop window. She was a dreamer, given to getting absorbed in her thoughts, standing gazing at her reflection in the glorious gilt mirror in the back shop. If her mother caught her, she would thunder towards her, screaming oaths about gutters and poorhouses, grab her, not always by the hair, and propel her to the door and the common stair leading to the shop where she was meant to be. To her mother's mind, any inactivity, and by that she meant reflection, dreaming, reading, signalled laziness.

My mother craved music all her life. At Mass, she sang the Latin responses in the manner of Billie Holliday. She went from thumping away on wood, all the while crooning to herself and imagining she was Bessie Smith, to later undertaking marriage to a saxophone player, Alec Argent, my father (talented, but a devoted drinker, which finally ended both his promising musical career and their marriage). Her most provocative habit was to play a dumb piano on the flat surfaces of the outers of sweets or boxes of wafers. It fell to Louise, her elder sister, the more practical of the two, to undertake most of the housework. Monday was family washing day. Louise was kept off school to fulfil the task. I can never remember, nor did I hear any tale of my grandmother doing housework. She was devoted to her shop and her till; a fine role model for the strong career women who were to succeed her. This enforced absenteeism from school for Louise, the denial of music for Cristina and the privileges given to their brother Rico, proved toxic for years to come. Louise, who died in her fifties of overwork and stress, but mainly of the worry that her realism and wisdom brought, never learned to read and write well. Rico had learned from what he saw daily and physically abused any female family member who did not do his bidding, including their and our poor 'Italian girls', home helps from Viticuso, me, and his depleted wife.

My grandmother's mood was often dark for so many reasons, but mainly because she never totally fell in love, I believe, with my grandfather. She had turned down Tony, left behind in Viticuso. Disillusioned maybe with marriage, the daily struggle of city life, a new language, and ways of being, anything that annoyed her would cause a violent scene, a hard slap on the face; normality among Italian families of the time. She was generally fearsome and it was hard to imagine her in any kind of delicto which led to her three children. She had her own view of men, there to serve her, there to obey but constantly seeking sexual satisfaction. There had been family secrets of her poor dishevelled husband, Emilio, appearing in his son's bedroom in the middle of the night, torn nightshirt and face bloodied in response to an amorous advance. While sex was by all accounts mostly denied, his wife became increasingly obsessed with where else he might be satisfying his 'animalistic' impulses: 'Men's dirt' she would say. However, my grandfather was in fact quiet, gentle and mild; a timid and sensitive man; loving, hard working and dutiful, especially to his wife. My mother was without any doubt his favourite. They were similar in temperament and she was both proud and vain, thereby charming her long-suffering father. She and her father, in tacit agreement and with the minimum provocation, rode the roaring storms of Italian life in a Scotland-based home with a mix of humour and resigned detachment.

On that summer's evening at eight o'clock, the phone rang. A voice my mother didn't recognise said 'Cristì', get out of there now. There's a mob movin' up the Walk and they're smashin' up a' the Italian shops. I'm no jokin' with ye... get out! We're at war wi Britain *e chiam' a Di' ch' c'aiud'*, may God help us now.'

Shaken and bewildered, my mother rushed out of the shop. Just as she got into the stair to their flat and closed the door, she heard the first sounds of breaking glass.

One of her greatest pleasures had been to collect and play jazz records in the café, which was open until late at night. People would come in out of the cold for a bit of fun; a bit of cheer during the deprivations of wartime. They wanted their coffee, Russian teas (tea in a long glass with a slice of lemon) or plates of hot peas and vinegar, which were popular at that time. Peas were not rationed after all. Once the music started from the old gramophone, people got up and started to dance; the quickstep, the hop and the waltz, if they were feeling a bit sentimental. Many a romance was begun in Shrubhill Café; many a falling for polka dots and silvery moons. For those were the days of the Bobby Soxers and a brilliantly fresh Frank Sinatra with a technique honed from the Dorsey horn and the dreams of a young going-places Sicilian. They were the days of the rough-smooth voice of Billie Holliday and the ephemeral and 'divine' (as my mother called him) Glenn Miller, his newly released 'Don't Sit Under the Apple Tree' and 'Moonlight Serenade' breathlessly brought in by Rico or her cousin Ernie Rossi, newly married with a shop in Loanhead.

My mother used to say that those were the happiest days of her life and I do believe it was an era of romance stolen at a time of fear, sweetened by uncertainty and inevitability; but it was a strange thing to say nonetheless, since the country was at war. And that night, her most treasured possessions, her jazz collection, along with the carefully polished sweetie jars, the tables and chairs bought one by one, the coffee machine and hand-rotated ice cream maker, were all destroyed by bricks, iron bars and fury. That was the night when the fate of every Italian family in Scotland turned. They became enemy aliens; and for many living in Scotland as unwelcome immigrants or on borrowed time, their family connections and how each family member was to another, irredeemably altered. I have one relic which survived; one remaining sweetie jar, its glass yellowed with age. It sits on a shelf in my lounge, my link to my grandfather.

There have been many accounts of that night in other narratives of the riots throughout Scotland and Britain, in Edinburgh, Glasgow, Clydebank; of terrorised Italian families, many of whom had taken British citizenship, barricading themselves in the back shop. I heard only recently of

three Glasgow children left in sole charge of the family business. The eldest was thirteen. Their father had been arrested
as an enemy alien. They describe standing at the window
watching while their mother, since wives were a threat to a
'protected' city, was taken off in a police car. Some families
were spared the devastation because of the individual loyalty
of friends and their local Scottish community. But the Rossi
family, homely Mary and not Mariuccia, the gentle moustached Meelie and not Emilio, for that was what the locals of
Leith called them, were in that one night transformed from
being a well-loved and honoured family into 'dirty Ities'.
Any unexpressed or historic racism, which had been tamed
through the necessity of communal living in hard times and
interdependence, finally found its voice. Historians are keen
to point out that anti-Italianism was in fact not something
of the moment, a response to the war announcement, but
that an undercurrent of racism towards Italian immigrants
had been present since the first mass arrivals in 1870. It was
a prejudice further added to by a general mood of anti-Ca-
tholicism.

My grandmother had shown remarkable foresight. She
had both the gift of foresight and second sight, knowing
through her dreams of the death of her brothers in the US
and her sisters in England. Her constant mantras were:
'Never speak loudly in Italian; we are guests in this country';
'Learn from those you see around you'; and 'Please, please
take British citizenship'. She as did many others, knew how
important it was for Italians to be as invisible as possible...
to be aware at all times that they were incomers; that things
could turn at any time. As she put it: *Di lavor in n' ora*, God
works in an hour. And on the night of the tenth of June, he
did. On the eleventh of June, and all through the following
night, every Italian household across Scotland and Britain
was raided by police.

Di Mambro, in her moving play *Tally's Blood*, describes

what happened: a household of fear... chanting outside of 'Get the Tallies'... a knocking at the door. It is two am. It's the police. There is joy and relief... finally, some law and order to protect them. But not so. General commotion ensues as police rush in, and rather than protecting the Pedreschi family from the rioters outside the door, they arrest Massimo, amidst pleading, clinging, many tears, and even reassurances... 'If we do as we're told we'll be alright'. Massimo returns at the end of the war after being transported to Canada, but his father perished on the *Arandora Star*. In other accounts, men are hauled from their beds where they are sleeping with their wives. There is barely sufficient time to get dressed. No explanations given. When I saw *Tally's Blood* many years later in the small Scottish town of Dunfermline, the murmur of weeping women in the audience... women who remembered... was almost more moving than what was happening onstage.

At this point in the story, things become confused and unclear. But what is now all too apparent to me is the desperate suffering of my family both in Viticuso and in Scotland. Like many peoples throughout history, Italians grasped a vision of a 'better life', of less hardship and of gaining the esteem of their neighbours. For most Italians, whether in Scotland or Italy, that vision was embodied in the power and eloquence of a dictator. Mussolini offered dignity and respect to a country which in the words of Dante had been '*serva Italia, non donna di provincia, ma bordello*': Italy as servant rather than genteel lady; a brothel, historically and repeatedly invaded, trampled on and subjugated. But in the days after the declaration of war on Britain by Italy, and the arrests of its citizens who were staunch in their loyalty and trust, no help or support came. Italian government officials who had encouraged summer camps and trips to Italy to see the great dictator, who had encouraged the beating romantic hearts of young women and made youths stand proud, who had organised local fascist clubs and dances, promoting an ideology of hope and trust, suddenly were not only silent, but completely absent.

In the ensuing days there was no one to turn to.

Viticuso, 1913 and 2005

At the golden gate of this sparse country
long emptied of its youth,
its finger games and hopscotch,
and where we sat, my daughters and I,
eating a handspun meal,
sipping red wine from lemonade bottles,
visited family, long ago interred in marble,
started at a photo of a woman we had once met
smiling out from her tomb under the weight
of a *mezzogiorno* afternoon;
where we saw an unclothed sun finally give itself up,
dipping its rim into those sweat sodden fields.
Was it here that my grandfather
ate his bread and sweet onions,
while resting his back at the angelus tolling?
Or here that he lay to capture the woman
who courted with tricks?
Here that she danced her *ballarella*,
hankie in hand for decency's sake?

And in leaving that dry, slow place,
and putting it back on the shelf
like an unfamiliar book we took down,
for this one day,
an odyssey to read together, maybe
like the Katie Morag tales that we once loved,
an accordion took us by surprise,
breathing life into that street,
as if replacing sunlight.
And I see
a clog-shod woman,

proud duchess that she was,
standing at the crossroads,
child at her skirts,
spun cloth across her back and legacy in her pockets,
about to turn the corner of her life,
bound for a land that would call her Mary;
a Leith street,
a new war not yet in the making,
cots for her children which smelt still of oranges
a hurdy gurdy, the salt and grit of a cream ice,
Italian delights and satin overalls,
white-gloved car rides to country hotels
 for a two week treat,
she leaves this land to the ghosts yet to come.

And today,
in the white sand of an untrafficked Hebridean island,
a lifeboat, lost 'Star' of Italy at its journey's end,
here and not there;
its load scattered like roses on the water,
their shaming call in the seas' tides.

The Sinking of the *Arandora Star*

THE ARRESTED MEN from all over the country were taken to Donaldsons School in Edinburgh, a makeshift prison; then, still wearing the same clothes that they had been arrested in, underfed, frightened and weary, they were taken to Liverpool. My mother and grandmother saw my grandfather only once in Donaldsons, six weeks after his arrest – and for the last time, though they did not know it. Shortly after the men arrived in Liverpool, like troubadours, Round Table knights with none of the glory, they were given access to priests, took communion and were finally loaded on to the *Arandora Star*. One account, among many, on the internet, reads as follows:

> The *Arandora Star* was a cruise ship that, like many others, had been requisitioned by the government for war use. Painted battleship grey, she had retrieved British troops after the fall of Norway in early June 1940, and played the same role later that month after the fall of France. She was designated to sail from Liverpool to Newfoundland, carrying 712 Italians, 478 Germans and 374 British guards and crew. Even though this was more than three times the peacetime occupancy, the number of lifeboats had not been increased. Layers of barbed wire were placed between decks. The Captain, EW Moulton, had protested, demanding the number of passengers be

halved and the barbed wire be removed, saying, 'If anything happens to the ship, that wire will obstruct passage
to the boats and rafts. We shall be drowned like rats and
the *Arandora Star* turned into a floating death-trap.' He
was overruled. At 4am on 1st July 1940, across the river from the Birkenhead shipyard that built her 14 years
earlier, the *Arandora Star* left Liverpool. She was unes-
corted, unmarked, and steamed at cruising speed. Had
she been painted with a red cross it would have been
apparent she was not on a military mission. As it was,
she looked like what she had so recently been, a troop
carrier. At 7am on 2nd July, north west of Ireland, a German U-boat spotted her and fired. The unarmoured ship
was deeply penetrated and took on water for just half an
hour before sinking.

In the late nineties, I went to see the film *Titanic* with my
husband and our three girls. My middle daughter, Roberta,
then twelve years old, was 'in love' with Leonardo di Caprio.
I still remember the sudden, unexpected choking feeling, my
trembling legs as I watched water pouring into the lower
decks, people running through the rising sea in kitchens,
corridors and sleeping quarters. It was the first time I had
felt any emotional connection to this event in my family
history. I was not on the *Arandora Star,* I have heard no
first-hand accounts of it, though there were some survivors,
I never knew my grandfather, but in those final moments
of the film an instinctive, lucid knowing overwhelmed me;
his terror, his vulnerability, his powerlessness faced with his
own death; rapid, jumbled snapshots of his life, of Leith,
of the mountains of Viticuso, his wife superb at that till in
Shrubhill Café; his son and two daughters; all were my own;
the force of his regret for not succumbing, not taking British
citizenship; his bewilderment left me gasping.

As the main protagonists in the film stand clinging to one another, waiting for the last surge; as the ship rears upwards, a final slicing through black water, all I could think of was my grandfather's terror-filled plunge into the Irish Sea. Through all the years since, I remain physically unable to endure any account of a mass drowning and in my search for any information, one version of events is almost unreadable still:

> I could see hundreds of men clinging to the ship. They were like ants and then the ship went up at one end and slid down, taking the men with her. Many men had broken their necks jumping or diving into the water. Others injured themselves by landing on drifting wreckage and floating debris near the sinking ship.
>
> (Sergeant Norman Price)

Rico had been born in Scotland and was therefore not in the front line but in the pioneer support core to the British army like many Italian sons. He has written his own moving and bizarre account of that early morning, which he entrusted to me not long before his own death. He found himself at a washbasin in the men's toilets around the time of the tragedy. Ignorant of the sinking, far from the scene and for no reason, as if struck by an unknown blow, he suddenly felt very unwell and broke into a cold sweat. The room swaying before his eyes, he collapsed on the floor.

A parallel monument to that of Mamma Ciociara, to the ill-fated *Arandora Star* and the five hundred Italian men lost at sea is now finally, and sadly only very recently, to be found in the courtyard of St Andrew's RC Cathedral in Glasgow, a place of dignity and repose in the city centre.

I still muse over the barbed wire which prevented escape; the shortage of lifeboats for the fifteen hundred or so men aboard of whom seven hundred and twelve were Italians; the sleeping bodies on the dining room floor of the boat; my grandfather reconciling with his brother Pietro Rossi, Ernie's father, after a twenty-year fall out and when it was clear that they had only minutes left to live. I see a moustached man, a gentleman by all accounts, standing on the deck, unable to swim, frightened in that way that the unworldly are afraid, erect in his formal black overcoat ... for the cold, for dignity... to meet his Maker? And despite the shouts from his fellow prisoners, refusing to 'Jump!Jump!'. There have been reports of shooting and of soldiers preventing escape, bullet holes in the lifeboats. Conjecture? Drama? Who knows?

Who knows too if there is any significance in the pull I have felt for some ten years or more towards the Scottish isles. They, more than anywhere, are where I am most happy in solitude, in a woolly hat, porridge and whisky in my panniers and a notebook in my rucksack. I have made it my business to visit them all with a tent, on a bike, by post bus and train, on ferries. And how I feel reminds me of one of my favourite poems in my teens: Wordsworth's 'Tintern Abbey': 'and I have felt a presence that disturbs me with the joy/ Of elevated thoughts; a sense sublime of something far more deeply interfused'.

The sandstone shelving at Duncansby Head, Rhum's Cuillins glowing red at dawn, the airy grasses of Berneray, the still, pale desert land of a North Uist beach, sandpipers busy among shells, the deliberate beat of the wings of a heron, these are images that infuse me with a sense of reconciliation primarily with myself; and strangely, it was on these islands, in that machair, on these beaches that the dead of the *Arandora Star* washed up. I did not know this until very recently when I visited Colonsay, where I was grandiosely and annoyingly escorted to the grave of a British soldier, for whom shamefully, I could feel no pity, only a lingering question as I looked down: 'What part did you play in that war crime?' For many years I have been urged by some force within me to return in simplicity and alone, again and again. And to come back into the city pacified.

I am grateful to a friend, Beth, who when I told her about this book, said, 'I sometimes wonder that the Scottish Italian community wanted to stay on here post-war. I remember my mum talking about the horror of what was done, and later, Italian friends and neighbours told me more. I am very glad that the Italian Scots did stay. Scotland is greatly enriched by the Italian community.' I was surprised and grateful too to BBC Radio Scotland who, amidst the celebration of Britishness and bravery, the pomp of Remembrance Sunday, in 2015 chose to feature the experience of Italians living in Scotland during World War Two. For this landmark report, tentative voices from the other side, (many Italian Scots are reluctant still to discuss the war), I am in a small way thankful.

If there was any discussion in my home about those events, I never heard it. That silence was offset by my early experience of Benny Goodman, Artie Shaw, Cab Calloway and the Hot Club of France, the magic of the Grappelli violin; music to get lost in, music to swallow you whole, music so visceral that it seems to pour out from inside you. This was one of my mother's gifts to me. Her way of coping with the tragedies of war was to disappear into that world of improvisation and syncopation, of *Lady Sings the Blues* and Satchmo, into a universe of fantasy. Her other gift to me was the love of books; Pearl Buck and H Rider Haggard, Louisa May Alcott, the Brontës. These were the only escape routes available to her, confined as she was by a tradition and system that even then I saw as unjust. I believe that my mother hoped that her Heathcliffe might suddenly show up one day on the Meadows when she was walking the dog. The continual fluctuations in the role and status of my family in post-war Scotland, I suppose, made a strong case for an anchoring. And so, the prime relationship in the family in the new order, with Grandad dead, became the one between Grandma and her married son, Rico. I was a silent witness to those mother and son strategic conversations, to the dictats given to my mother, and I agonised, felt grossly impotent at being a voiceless child. I raged at my mother's servility and my own inability to defend her or raise her up. I saw her negated.

My own journey of gradual detaching, of great care in what I committed to, of cool objectivity, of identifying with both sides to the point sometimes of not knowing what to think, my tendency to critique and question, my passionate articulation of distinction and difference, most of all my rejection of norms, and my lifestyle fashioned not on what I saw, but what seemed natural, started then.

Italian Odyssey

It is 1st July 1940, off the West Coast of Ireland.

He is breathing cargo
and still wearing the reek
of twenty-one days in a cell
he is a traveller again, peaceable and without baggage.
Or sin.
There had been a visitor, late in the night
 but was this a time for host or any sacrament?

Before him, in the late evening
a cruise ship, *Arandora Star*
proud in her dock,
her deck now laced with metal
a crowning with thorns.
Mother for all ages, taking to her belly,
all seven hundred... sellers of hams, sweeties and flowers,
her dance room floor is soft with boys and men
the air stale with uncertainty.

Then at sometime around seven am,
a last fling of a passing German boat
 a torpedo, the spider's bite,
a danse macabre in full fatal swing,
the sliding slowing
he holds a brother close, a first in twenty years,
 'Jump! Jump!',
but there had been no sea in Lazio,
he stands erect, overcoated, elegantly poised.

The stranger's arrival is swift.

Highlights: Early Influences

A Contentious Marriage

MY MOTHER AND father married in April 1943 when Italy
and Britain were at war and my grandfather had drowned
as an enemy alien less than three years before. Only now
do I realise the huge import of this action. My mother had
always been very clear that she would not marry another
Italian. She flouted the prevailing system of family approval,
of community dances and social get-togethers, had little
patience with gatherings where that new generation of
Italians born in Scotland were encouraged to meet their
prospective partner in innocence and where it was hoped
they would establish a contained, well-policed courtship.
Those few who sought love outside the community were the
butt of gossip. They were seen to be morally free, which was
acceptable as far as men were concerned, encouraged even,
but not for women.

There existed a well recognised practice of much of the
contact between boy and girl taking place within the families
of both or within the wider Italian community. It was brave
for any individual from the community to bring a native
Scot to that tight group, so much of that relationship would
be conducted elsewhere, thus further fuelling speculation.
The parameters of these marriage arrangements were mainly
economic security, collateral, a family business, 'solidity'
and a known family history. As for women, the qualities that
mattered were modesty, support of her prospective husband

47

and freedom from any prior entanglements. Women were judged on whether they were hard workers and whether too, they possessed the wherewithal for motherhood and home-making. These were the criteria for suitability.

I have attended many weddings within the community over the years. I have married within it and observed many newly weds. What is striking in the Italian community of today and of the years when I was growing up, is the emphasis on family rather than on passion or love, or on a relationship between existing lovers or lovers in the making. There is a tendency among the parents of the couple to speak of them as their own, pure, untainted children within an existing economic structure, at work and at play, who will in time, somehow, seductively, secretively and surreptitiously extend the family network. This I believe stands in stark contrast to weddings of Scottish people, where there lurks a realistic awareness of the sexuality of both parties, of the pleasures and fun of sex. There is a light-hearted explicitness in the bawdiness of the speeches and jokes. In Italian circles on the other hand, that major step of choosing a life partner because of love or sexual compatibility is neither alluded to, nor considered. If passion is indeed present, though I have often wondered about that, the obligation is to keep it for the bridal suite, and often these things take time. The most daring aspect of these weddings is to this day an intermittent chant from the coy crowd of *'bacio, bacio, bacio, bacio'* and the blushing kissing response. Further evidence perhaps of Italian marriage as primarily a practical, economic arrangement, and maybe also a throwback to village life, is for the newly conjoined couple to visit the family the day after the wedding and their first night together – my own experience.

In reflecting on these conventions, many of which still persist, what I understand of my mother is that unlike her siblings and contemporaries, she was an unrepentant, devoted romantic; subtly and sexually driven, passionate and resourceful in her loving and her approach to life. I know these aspects of my mother's personality not so much through confidences that she shared with me (she would often declare, not without some drama, 'You don't know me' and I don't think I ever really did), but through listening to her and observing her as she struggled to lead the life she wanted and not the one that was continually imposed on her.

Her secrets however, usually emerged in her emotional outbursts at any behaviour of mine that hinted at my transition to womanhood. This included the first time I wore a bra, lipstick or tights. Her expression on those occasions – I thought that the best approach was to appear discreetly anew, rather than discuss the matter – filled me with anxiety that some awkward scene would take place. She railed at my choice of men; sobbed in despair at my decision to marry and to 'leave her alone'. 'What will I do now? Who will I go on holiday with?' she shouted in dismay when Paul and I broke the news that we planned to marry, after a seven-year courtship. Indeed, my year-long engagement was mainly conducted in secrecy: gifts handed to me while she was out of the room; congratulations muted; the subject avoided in her presence.

Wedding arrangements were made by Paul and me, giddy with worry and fear, picking up clues, learning as we went. It was my future sister-in-law, Joanna, who helped me to choose the wedding dress that my mother never saw until my wedding day; and I paid for it myself with an arranged overdraft from my bank manager, who I successfully charmed. Relying solely on skills acquired through our respective careers as a teacher and a solicitor, together with Paul's activities in politics and mine in music and choral work, we ploughed on and into a wedding day that my mother attended, collapsing in grief when we left the reception.

It was in a rare moment of honesty then, permitted only

to her and never to me, for I never dared discuss my relationships in any depth, that she referred to my father's lovemaking as considerate and beautiful; him as golden.

She wanted no part of the coupling rituals of her heritage and of this I feel greatly proud. That she had the courage to step outside, challenge norms and have the confidence to infiltrate another culture and a more liberal set of norms than her own, is to her credit, particularly as it was intensely shocking to do so at that period in the history of Italians living in Scotland. To pursue glamour, emulate Hedy Lamarr, be fascinated by the androgeny of Marlene Dietrich, style herself as a Loren in that closed Italian value system, required the creative energy, open-mindedness, and independence of spirit of a self-styled woman in a bygone, anachronistic world. Her actions represented a stubborn deviation from the behaviour of other young Italian women, for she could not or refused, to cook and clean, preferring her dialogues with the mirror, her imaginings through music, books and Canaletto or the Gainsburgh ladies, to the drudgery of the shop counter and the till. Her activities outside the Italian community were a challenge to her equally determined mother and her controlling brother, the new head of the family.

Her romance and subsequent marriage to an RAF serviceman under the ultimate command of Churchill, who had ordered the 'collaring' and internment of all Italian men in Britain over the age of sixteen, and the recent death of her own father on the *Arandora Star*, was it can only be said both deliberately provocative and audacious. It was indeed outrageous. Flirtatious and 'painted' were how her family and that conventional community saw my mother. For my part I bow to her spirit in crossing the line, to her grasp of a world beyond, and keeping her eye on the opportunities of the post-war years and the wider social and cultural context of which the Italian 'colony', as it was called then, was, she recognised, only one small element.

Her route to that hasty marriage is not entirely clear; her ways of meeting and being with my father, sadly, never recounted. There is maybe much that I could have learned in relation to my own relationship experience. But I remember her later in her life both as a vamp, dark haired, seductive and curvaceous, making careful preparations for her entry through the doorway of The Copper Kettle café in Bruntsfield, no earlier than eleven, the shop in full busyness, schoolchildren clamouring at the counter. At the same time, I experienced her as increasingly disapproving of my womanhood and my mounting confidence in my own powers of attraction. I generally managed to maintain an equilibrium in our adult relationship by adopting a neutral persona, devoid of sexuality, mainly as a mother; any glamour acceptable if merely cosmetic, and never alluring. She did of course attend the Italian dances, weddings and *Fascio* gatherings as a young girl, but my guess is that like many of her generation, her participation was certainly not political. While romance in her heart ebbed with despair at the honest, young, second-generation Italian men and the settled shop life they offered, it flamed ever more strongly in the clubs, the jazz venues, the daring drinks and dances of Edinburgh's night life where she first met Alec Argent.

My father, Alec, a saxophone player and clarinettist, was well-known in the Edinburgh clubs and dance halls. He eventually achieved a seat in the Geraldo Orchestra, a well-known big band of the 1940s, and later the offer to play in the well-regarded Ted Heath orchestra, which he never took up, I think because of his unreliability. I remember watching television with my mother and grandmother in the late 1950s, after he had left Edinburgh, and once or twice spotting him among the front desks of the Geraldo brass section.

Alec was as alien to the community of Italians as Italian

tradition was to him. Had he been willing to integrate and learn Italian ways, appropriate new and what was believed to be better values, become a steadfast, hard-working brother and son-in-law, things might have been different. But as a working-class Scot and a musician, the overt disapproval of the marriage both by my grandmother and my uncle was matched in intensity by his own obdurate attitude. I did not know him, but I know this instinctively.

Those were the days when the Catholic Church demanded that anyone marrying a Roman Catholic was required either to embrace that religion, or in practice, value it above their own. Though he had no attachment to any other religion, Alec did not convert to Roman Catholicism. So my mother and father were not permitted to marry at the main altar of St Mary's RC Catholic Cathedral in Leith Walk, but in the vesting room, the sacristy, the annex to it. It is telling that there are no photographs of the wedding, nor have I heard any accounts of it. The only evidence of its legality is the marriage certificate and the divorce papers. One could say that disapproval of the match came from every quarter.

The concept of being owned within an Italian family, especially as a woman, was a major factor in the failure of that marriage; that and the clash of one culture against another. There was no licence for the new couple to build something together, because Cristina remained a Rossi, possibly in her heart, and certainly in the eyes of her family. Given space, differences could have been harmonised and a new culture harnessing both traditions created by the couple. Quite possibly too, my mother, after what was probably seen as folly and disloyalty, was anxious to appease. Or maybe she already recognised the unachievable; two opposed paradigms wrought on the one hand from the deprivations and frustrations of a bloke from Bangholm, who used to climb out of his bedroom window at night to get to the clubs and play his music; on the other, from an immigrant family made vulnerable by recent events, clutching at any opportunity to find solid ground. This was a family with its eye on a respectable, middle-class way of life. Or maybe, as life became more difficult financially, an income from music and car dealing, my mother began to value what she had previously rejected. Cristina's brother and her older sister Louise, now married into the Coletta family, with its reputation for ice cream and catering in Blackpool, made strenuous efforts at the start, after Alec returned from service post-war, to involve him in the family businesses: in my grandmother's café, The Copper Kettle; my uncle's ice cream shop in Morningside; and, in the Coletta empire on the Fylde Coast in Lancashire. All were unsuccessful. The fact that they married in the war years also meant that my father was away from home for extended periods. Ironically, some of that time was spent in Italy.

My mother and father went for a short time to live in a bed and breakfast in Blackpool, returned to Edinburgh and in the end settled down to live with my grandmother in her flat in Morningside, my mother, it seemed, finally capitulating to mounting pressures on both sides, acquiescence and indecision, an unwillingness to take further risks. These were character traits which contradicted the bold step of her marriage and which I only saw consistently in relation to men, to her brother and husband. My father expressed his smouldering anger and ultimate rejection of the Rossi family through whisky and drunkenness. He did sometimes, I am told, spend time with his brother-in-law, Rico, but generally the arrival of family members, most especially from Blackpool, signalled his immediate departure from the house to the pub. His sorties to the Miller's Arms were his haven from Rossi family life.

Like geysers in a geothermal field, eruptions through the compression of the spoken and unspoken were sometimes predictable, more often unpredictable, always dramatic and increasingly devastating. This then was the scenario of my early years. Whenever I was alone with my father I had a strong sense of being with a stranger, with a man I didn't know, and I longed for security and the familiar; for my mother or my grandmother to come back soon. He was a reluctant caretaker of his daughter, a mysterious visitor in our home. Because I didn't know him, I was unsure and wary of his reactions. Above all, I tried hard not to irritate or anger him. I sensed his detachment and rancour, and what I felt, even possibly remembered, his potential for violence. I don't remember him ever speaking to or engaging with me but I remember one evening when he was at home. It was one rare evening when we prepared to eat together as something resembling a family. My mother was in the kitchenette making tea and he was keeping me busy while we waited. Recognising the signals of escalating impatience, leading to anger towards me, a small child, my mother suddenly appeared holding a pan of hot fat: 'If you lay one finger on her, I'll pour this all over you,' she said.

I have a memory of being left with him one cold, shadowy Sunday morning; a memory one afternoon of creeping into the box-room where I saw the parts of his clarinet and saxophone neatly stored in black casing, his black jacket and trousers, a bow tie; his work attire. And I remember a tense, wordless evening with my mother and father on either side of a coal fire, my father's eye on the clock, his quick escape before pub closing time at ten. The final chapter for me, but not for my mother, came one night in winter when I was six years old.

The kitchen/living area was brightly lit, the wallpaper brown. We had tea. My grandmother had retired to her bedroom at the front of the house and my mother was buttoning up my dressing gown before putting me to bed in the room across the corridor, the room shared by my mother and father, where I slept in my mother's bed. I had sensed a tension in her all evening. She was emotional, preoccupied.

Then I heard a key in the front door and the kitchen door opened behind me. My mother became stiff, a strange look in her eyes. I remember being puzzled. I kept my eyes on her. I didn't look behind. No words were spoken. She led me through to bed and my father followed. She tucked me up and kissed me. My eyes were now on my father, just inside the door, standing behind her. I seemed to know what would happen next. Maybe I had seen it all before, I have no idea. What I do know is that any memories of my early years are random and few. My mother turned around to leave the room. He struck her hard. I don't remember any sound from her. Was she used to it? Should I have warned her? I certainly had seen the danger. I knew the plan. She was defenceless, soft and vulnerable as she bent over me. Yet I had done nothing to stop it. I started to scream, jumping up and down on the bed, and heard the heavy advance of my grandmother through the hallway. With no hesitation, with her full strength, she lashed out and knocked him down. It was easy. He was drunk.

I remember blood on his hand as he scraped it on my little basket chair at the foot of the bed. I have no other memory. I can't remember what he, or my mother or grandmother did next. I seem to remember him not getting up from the floor. I think later there was a photograph of a woman taken from the pocket of his jacket, which was hanging over the back of a chair in the kitchen. My mother looked at it, put it back and I took it out again to see. Then, suddenly there were men in the kitchen, the doctor and my uncle, and then my father. Someone, possibly my mother, took me across the landing to the door opposite and tried to make me stay with Miss Thomson but I wouldn't, and so I was put into my grandmother's bed in a dark, cold room. I felt confused, forgotten though safe, and wondered what would happen now. I also felt strangely satisfied that my father had been knocked down by my grandmother; by her taking control.

It was the first time I had had the feeling of vengeance. I felt darkly triumphant, that his violence had been matched by violence, that my mother had been finally championed, that he had been cut down. Something major had been achieved. I heard voices, couldn't make out what was being said. I heard the front door close. I ran to the window and looked out at the street. My father was standing looking back up at the windows. I felt no sadness or loss, only a relief that I cannot account for. I went back to bed. I didn't see him again.

The Man Who Was My Father

The dark man whose voice I can't recall
who was my father
offered me a boiled egg
one Sunday morning when it wasn't sunny
and you had left for Mass
when the gas hob in our ration-book scullery was still
the pots, our story books of roots and rooting
of Italy and immigration, not needed,
they held their breath
and the bread bin where you kept the few pounds
my father couldn't find, kept your secret.

I can't recall if it was the yolk or the white
that I couldn't eat, or why,
but I can recall a room the colour of fudge
but without its sweetness
a tenement window which kept out the light
stale grass of our shared green below
the daily drudge of a pulley,
my oversized cot a barren place.

And for the first time that morning I tasted frozen
like the chill on your face at some later time
at the opening of a door somewhere behind me
the draught of air that blew fear into your eyes
uncertain into mine as you did up my buttons
put me to bed, kissed me goodnight,
and I didn't feel safe,
and I saw him behind you, waiting
for you to turn round,
for the fairy tale to finish.

I can still see him now after...
your tears, the police and people...
standing on the pavement below
in standard gaberdine,
dance hall lights behind,
the man who was my father.

The Power of an Italian Grandmother

FROM MY GRANDMOTHER, with whom I slept from the age of six until my early teens, I learned a great deal. I did this more by watching and listening to her. 'If it wasn't for me you'd be in the gutter,' she would say to me and to my mother. Her loving distant, she was never tender, but she cared for me and I spent a lot of my time with her. As a child I had a growing sense of womanhood: of both the strong in her and the denied in my mother; of traditional roles allocated and imposed on the one hand and the power and potential of woman on the other. My grandmother commanded; my uncle acted; my mother obeyed, living *co' du per renda na scarp'* (with two feet in one shoe), in other words, timidly. Rico worshipped one woman, his mother; he disrespected all others.

An important influence for me from birth was the southern, *laziale* Italian dialect, the *viticusar* of my grandmother, and with it a way of seeing the world. It is an altogether different language to standard Italian; it brings a different lens on people, their habits and purposes. That was the language I heard around me and spoke with Grandma. The dialect was a seedbed for the ease I have with foreign languages and the extent to which a language for me is more than a technical skill. The ingestion of another language which has more to do with feeling and instinct offers new possibilities for identity. Together with English, the dialect was my first language, the language of familiarity and home. Even today, when I get the chance of speaking that dialect though it sits incongruously with how I present now, I find that other, truer identity. It brings with it more honesty and humour. It brings a pragmatic understanding of human nature: *facenner,* busybody, hyperactive woman; *ne fesse,* gullible; *cornud,* womaniser; *man' sciode,* deft; *na lamentos,* a moaning woman. And some good practical advice: *fa ben e scordate, fa mal e pensace,* forget the good that you do and reflect on the wrongs; *chi spud nell'aria, gle reve n' facce,* if you spit in the air, it comes back on your face.

It seems to have opened a consciousness of and entry to a different language system and the real heart of words, despite their various manifestations in the different Romance languages, dialects and tenses. Whenever I came across an unfamiliar word at school in French, and later in Spanish, even Portuguese and oddly, Catalan, though I cannot claim to speak Spanish, or any version of it and far less Portuguese, it seemed as if I had always known the word. There was rarely a need to write it down and once heard I remembered it. I feel a deep affinity with conditional tenses and instinctively know how they should sound. This linguistic and cultural empathy and fluidity, and the different identities which I inhabit and present when travelling in Southern Europe, even in Greece, even where I pass at the very least, for Mediterranean, comes I believe from the language I learned in those post-war years in an Italian home.

At primary school with mainly Scottish girls, I had a strong sense of difference which I neutralised often by silence, watchfulness and choosing to remain peripheral; verbalising most often in writing. Strong friendships came later, as a teenager and as an adult when closeness began to matter. To this day however, I generally remain hugely shy, am often overwhelmed, sometimes rendered speechless and inarticulate by the strength of someone else's presence.

I mainly find my voice through the calmly written word in cool, thoughtful solitude. In total contradiction, what causes me the most pain is to be ignored, which sometimes leads me conduct myself in irrational ways in order to elicit a response and respect. I took care not to establish a connection with the Italian or Polish children in my class. I was a reluctant Italian. I kept my distance. The Italians I went to school with remain unaware of how culturally close we really are. My Scottish surname was both my camouflage and my opportunity.

The voice that drove me then (I still hear it), was mainly my grandmother's. Despite her frustration at her inability to read and write; she was an intelligent woman and an able businesswoman. A woman who was Mary from Bonnington Road where they started out wheeling an ice cream cart, she became the dignified lady who would in Jenners tea room be both known and respected. In those post-war years, as the lady in the hat, evocative of a Colourist portrait, Sir Will Darling himself would greet her in his Princes Street department store, where he would rush to get her a seat.

To 'be respected' was her compass; to be valued, a position earned not through any vulgar display of wealth but through the power of letters and education. Education, as Paolo Freire defined it for the Brazilian people in much of his writing, was literacy, democracy and power. That was how my grandmother regarded it too: emancipation, independence and freedom, the best means of moving forward in the world. Her inability to read and write was an obstacle to her achieving what she knew she was truly capable of. Through the lack of literacy, she was ultimately impotent, having to rely on others to read her letters, deal with the doctor, solicitors and banks. Remembering her struggling to write her own name on her pension book at the post office every month, I know now that hers were the values that formed and fired me. '*Fatte' maestr' mamà*'

(Be a teacher) she used to say, and I did begin a career in education as a teacher. This belief in education and its ability to transform and raise us, to win and require respect, has been my guide throughout my life.

Sunday mornings in Morningside were, as I remember them, sunny. That must have been after my drunken father was eventually bundled out the door. But I could never share at school how they were; could never reply when the inevitable questions arose about what we did on Sundays and did we go to Mass. I was as silent on the 'disgrace' of marital breakdown as I was about the glorious smell of *sugo* for Sunday spaghetti and our irregular attendance at Mass.

Although adherence to Church rules was not an imperative in our broadly Catholic home. Grandma did treat priests and the religious with respect. She would offer food or a whisky at any time of the day or evening. I have strong memories of coming home to find a priest sitting chatting with her and having a dram or two mid-afternoon. Religious belief, for Grandma, was fear and fate, appeasement, retribution and the sense of an all-seeing eye. She had her own favourite curse, of course: *'Te pozze schiattà'* (May you burst). Fortunately none of her targets did actually implode or indeed burst. She also had a fear of the power of *'gle mal'oiche'*, 'the evil eye'. In order to break the spell of the 'evil eye', she would put rice grains into a basin of water and and determinedly 'drown' with her thumb, any grains floating on the surface; the *mal'occhio* had been well dealt with for the time being.

Grandma did not have a wide cooking repertoire. She had come, after all, from a place where people survived on *pan' e cipoll'*, bread and onions; pasta, bread, garlic, potatoes, lentils. On special days a chicken's throat would be cut, the skinny bird cooked and brought to the table. There were pigs too, often becoming family pets, but these were valuable and sold for slaughter when the time came. From my grandmother I learned the importance of generosity.

There was never too much food. If there were no leftovers, she had not fed her family enough. I saw her often cooking a *frittata* for an unexpected visitor at eleven at night, whereas at that time of night, in a Scottish home, you might be lucky to get a cup of tea. For her, a welcome was the offer of food and drink. They were her currency. She made people feel warm and happy, and so they came often. I also learned that Christmas and New Year in an Italian home were about family. I do not remember wine or indeed alcohol. There clearly was wine, but it was of little importance. But I also learned something else. Every family needs a heart and a hearth. When Grandma, Zi' Mariucc', died no one else took on that role. But the instinct to offer my family and friends a place of good fare and fun has been a role I have carried through my own life. Family cafés opened for a half day or for as long as there was business to be done, on Christmas Day, and so our lunches were staggered, with people coming and going. New Year was a full day of opening. But nonetheless, I remember preparations for these days of family celebrations; Grandma and Ernestina, working in the kitchen; chickens, roasted and boiled, spaghetti, *bracciol* (beef olives); and never a turkey or a dessert though maybe there was indeed jelly and ice cream, our trademark as Italians, for us children. At New Year my mother's cousin Ernie, from Loanhead, would be at the door with his guitar and a lump of Scottish coal.

Parcels to and from Viticuso were a feature of upcoming celebrations, meaning that we were able to eat Italian food at a time when it was impossible to find it here in Scotland, nor could we request it, such was the burden of the past war and the limits imposed by ration books. But we were blessed with the arrival of sausages cured and made in Viticuso and sent by Zi' Nicandro, my grandmother's cousin and brother of Gnor' Zi', a Monsignor of the Church of whom Grandma was fiercely proud. Those amazing boxes also brought *baccalà,* salt cod; walnuts and dried figs. In return, we sent tea and hot chocolate, sugar and chocolate bars, for it was the aftermath of war and moreover, it was Southern Italy. My grandmother never lost her ties with the country; she made pizza with olive oil, garlic and fresh tomatoes, never cheese. She bought rennet from the chemist to make her own ricotta and would occasionally persuade Rico to drive to a farm where she would buy two live chickens, put them in the boot of the car where they clattered and clucked all the way home; and disposed of them at the back of the house with a pair of scissors. I can still see bloodstains on the paving stones at the back of our Bruntsfield flat. She would then gut them in the kitchen sink, a gruesome, smelly task, remove the feathers and hang the birds between two dining chairs to rid them of any residual blood and fluids. That done, they were ready for the pot. I still remember the wonder of Scamorza when it arrived from Italy and the little balls of butter embedded within those waxen, kidney-shaped cheeses.

A Family and Community in Transition

ERNESTINA ARRIVED IN Edinburgh from Viticuso in 1958. She was eighteen years old. My uncle went to Viticuso to collect her. I woke up early one morning to find this dark, forbidding looking stranger in my grandmother's bedroom. She stood barely in the door, slightly to our left. She spoke no English, her hair was caught up in a fat round bun, she wore quality grey suiting, which I imagine had been bought and tailored especially for the occasion, and no bra. It was not unusual during the fifties for Italian families to request a home help from their native village, and the whole operation was handled within the family networks that extended back across to Italy. Again, this was not something we spoke of to our Scottish neighbours. So, Rico's family had Amelia and we had Ernestina. The work for them was heavy, particularly in my home, for we had no washing machine, no fridge, and coal fires which had to be cleaned and set every day. In order to learn English, Ernestina also helped out in The Copper Kettle.

These were strong, hardy girls used to working the fields, women who made bread and pasta for the daily meals; who fed, bled and cleaned the animals they shared their night shelter with; women who helped with birthing and laying out the dead of their families, who built walls and repaired the roof after a storm. Compared to the devastation caused by the war in Lazio and by the frequent earthquakes and tremors native to that region, life in Edinburgh, tough as it was, still represented an opportunity. To come from Viticuso to an Italian family in Scotland was a chance for Ernestina to make something of her life, to be educated, polished in the ways of a city, make a marriage, be a *signora*.

She told many stories about her life in Viticuso. I liked the ones about her school experience best; about her teacher Don Cocó; a gentle, lumbering man burdened with the unwelcome task of teaching spirited, unwilling children to read and write. He lisped curses at his class of untameable tricksters wielding a large stick and vowing to *la Maronn'*, the Holy Virgin, the most extreme physical punishments. But he rarely caught them and things generally died down. Ernestina and her classmates found his clumsy attempts, together with his halting delivery, a fine treat, an incitement to even more devilry, resulting in further entertainment. Neither were they unaccustomed to beatings with whatever came to hand by whoever felt it was deserved. In the villages at that time children lived by *gle baston'*, the stick, survived the beatings, and took it in good part.

Nonetheless, Don Cocó and Ernestina had been respectively effective, for unlike many of her peers, Ernestina arrived in Scotland able to read and write in Italian rather than in dialect and she later went on to teach herself to read English, though not to write it. She was a skilful tailor, a natural cook, a lover of quality with a strong instinct for business investment and an appetite for both gambling and risk (she was often lucky on the roulette tables. I was not, though I loved the glamour of it of course). I had grown up in my own world, increasingly in my bedroom, a world of Hollywood and Frank Sinatra, the Rat Pack, Cole Porter and jazz clubs. I used to love in my twenties leaving the shop, and dressing in glamorous clothes for a late night session in Edinburgh's Carriage Club. But I have a clear albeit dismal memory of driving home in the wee small hours of Monday, another hard-earned twenty pounds lost, an early train to Glasgow, where I chose to spend my first year of teaching, ahead of me.

Ultimately liberated from the confines and narrowness of my family, late in life, Ernestina became a successful businesswoman and owner of a number of high earning properties. It was an astonishing achievement. This was the wide-eyed young woman for whom running water in the home had been a miracle, as indeed was a toilet and a whole room even given over to it. *Sott' la macer,* under a tree, was generally how people went about their regular business. I remember visiting my relatives in Viticuso in 1967 when flushing was still a matter of throwing a bucket of water down the toilet. In fact, it was still several years before water was plumbed into every property. Ernestina followed my grandmother's advice, as I would do later. She seized the opportunity given to her; firstly she learned the rudiments, the refinements of language and behaviour of the middle classes, for that was the aspiration of my own family; it was that accent, those speech mannerisms and those ways we made our own. Watchful, intelligent, Ernestina listened, especially to me as I moved successfully through the education system, and she also came to know the value of a university education. She observed advancement; she understood financial security; saw thrift and hard work as the means to it.

The arrival of Ernestina in my home as a survivor of the atrocities of war – who knows what she had seen and suffered, for she spoke of Moroccan troops with marked terror in her eyes – together with the renegotiation of our position in Edinburgh life as former enemy aliens, confirmed my home joyfully and shamelessly as an Italian one. We were also a family and a community in transition and this status of journeying, seeking and hoping to arrive finally, persisted until well into my adult life. Even in the seventies, we were the object of post-war insults and negativity. It was all around us. I guess that prejudice was present in the homes of many of my school friends, though I was unaware at the time. The insults landed over the shop counter, in the street and even in the playground, leaving me shocked, bewildered and often angry. My mother, Ernestina and Grandma shouldered them with resignation, having seen worse. In the workplace, partnership in a legal firm was withheld, reportedly, because of a name. That prejudice within the Edinburgh establishment and professional classes which we encountered was all the more insidious and damaging because it was subtle and unspoken; yet politely, firmly enacted. My husband and I felt honoured, had a sense of 'arrival', to get an invitation to an Edinburgh establishment dinner, to be asked to join a group to attend a charity ball; and it was essential to fit in, not to shock and to be mild at all times. Those who were more lenient towards our Latinate aspect were, I suppose, gladdened when the fact of it did not contaminate or intrude.

Fortunately for all concerned, those jibes at those I was close to throughout my childhood and adult years were never directed at me, because of my Scottish name and because I was careful to distract from my Italianism. But I heard and saw it. I fumed at it and on one occasion, at sixteen years old, pursued a man down the street who had insulted my mother over the price of an ice cream cone.

We continually countered these behaviours in silence and in our minds, and in the privacy of our homes with biting humour. We developed a counter-narrative of criticism and disdain of Scottish ways. This defence and reinforcement of our own proud Italian identity is still deeply rooted. It was with amusement that we sold chocolate to our Scottish customers, those enormous 'selection boxes' to guilt-ridden husbands, a peace offering for their wives, as they wended their way home after a Friday or Saturday night in the pub.

'They can't get enough of it', we said. *Magn' cioccolad,* chocolate eaters, was my grandmother's label for someone she considered unmanly; such an attachment to biscuits and sweet things! While our café menu ('give them what they want') consisted of variations around chips as a staple, we scornfully gloried in pasta, smoked fish with olive oil and garlic, believing in careful food preparation and confused at a Scottish reliance on frying, butter, lard and tins.

Around this time, there was the first appearance of Knorr chicken noodle packet soups in my home. I remember the simple joy of tinned spam, the glossy jelly of tinned pork meat; beans on toast, though I really preferred late night beans on their own, Cheyenne-cowboy style; and eventually Mary Baker (not Mary Berry) cake mixes; Bird's custard with tinned pears. Rich tea and Digestive biscuits found their way even into my Italian home. It also occurs to me that we never observed the Italian tradition of the major meal being eaten on Christmas Eve, and it was on Christmas Day, at that time hardly observed in Scotland, that we had our celebration. But it has never been turkey, but rather pasta with a *sugo* that had been nurtured for hours, the meat removed from it and served separately with salad. If there were vegetables such as Brussels sprouts or broccoli, they were first blanched before being sautéed in garlic and olive oil.

The small changes to what and how we ate at home due to a Scottish influence were partnered with the aroma of fried whitebait, begged or pre-ordered from the fishmonger; capons stuffed with forcemeat consisting of Italian sausage, garlic, raisins and breadcrumbs; camomile tea; broth with pasta and the discarded parts of the chicken (I particularly remember the brown scaly meat of the neck); fish coated in home-made breadcrumbs; eggs fried in olive oil; and the first Moka coffee-maker, brought straight from Italy by my uncle. We learned to make chips too, but an altogether better version was potatoes sautéed with onions and garlic.

An Appraisal and Matters of Choice

AS I GREW, I came to value certain Italian attitudes above how we understood those of Scottish society and I have to admit that this still remains the case. The sixties were the days of *cinecittà*, Loren, Lollobrigida, Fellini, Mastroiani, glamour and romance. We read *Oggi*, the old-time equivalent of *Hello*. It was an inspiration and an affirmation. The belief that Ernestina showed as a girl from a village in good quality tailoring was and is endemic to the Italian psyche. Despite the still limited resources of the post-war era, despite my conviction that there should be an honesty in how we present to the world, I could not help but increasingly notice and admire the efficiently elegant and careful presentation of my own community compared to the dull ragtag of what I saw around me in Edinburgh. Attention to how we looked was a strong factor, certainly for the women in my family. I learned it then and I live it now. There has never been a day when I have reached for just anything to wear and gone out on the street; nor a night when my last thought has not been what I will wear to present myself to the world tomorrow.

Normal daily interactions in my home were usually dramatic whereas in Scottish homes I saw calm, polite routine, a pervading sense of containment, which offer rest and respite, a welcome antidote; but for me, they were and are not sufficient in a life and at times I crave the unreasonable, the unexpected, the hot blaze of emotion.

I grew up with a cruel, unfettered directness, hard truths, often highly personal, delivered in anger, with some degree of violence, and which might result in some long-term family feud. Sometimes such a breach would heal at the very last as in the case of my grandfather with Pietro, his brother, on the sinking *Arandora Star* but very often not. Or there would be a reconciliation which might last for short periods, with highly charged meetings descending into chaos. In my wider family, there remains much that is unresolved and finally I have decided not to engage at all. Yet I have always felt that natural urge, which is my culture, for the same honesty with colleagues, in relationships and friendships. This has, not surprisingly, caused me many problems, not least throughout my career. I have truly felt that diplomacy was a waste of time; less than honest, in fact. My family practice of *na buon sfogad,* getting it off your chest, has always seemed to me best.

Where I placed myself in my formative years and later was therefore conflicted. While I had a strong attachment and loyalty to many values from my home culture, there were other values, attitudes and lifestyle which I saw outside the home and considered to be better.

I came to realise in my early teenage years that the pathway to a better position in society was education, and to see culture and the arts as a means of developing the intellect. So when I was old enough to be allowed to go my own way during the day, I went regularly to the music and art sections of the Central Library on George IV Bridge in Edinburgh. Here I would wander amazed and excited as I followed up on an author or poet mentioned by someone at school. In order to continue my journey of education and of respectability, I chose my friends carefully, those I felt I could learn from. I bought a season ticket for Friday night classical music concerts and spent my pocket money and later my student grant on solo excursions to shows and performances in the Edinburgh Festival, often four or five a day. I did not want company on these missions for they represented my private life. I had to work at appreciating a music very different to that of my upbringing, a different idiom; to cataloguing in my mind the key artists, sculptors, architects of the Western world. There were one or two teachers at school who saw my growing interest and encouraged me. I remember the first time I heard Schubert's Trout Quintet, in my sixth year at school. I was totally thrilled by it. My French teacher encouraged me to attend concerts and would often put records of classical music my way. Through her, I found Menotti and Prokofiev. However, it was my piano teacher who made the greatest contribution to my journey. This is how I described my connection with her in an article in *The Scottish Educational Review*:

Throughout a childhood, where my mother would have had more freedoms without me, my relationship as a thirteen-year-old with an adult, my piano teacher, who spoke to me, was interested in how I felt, could somehow intuit my unexpressed, and not only guess at but create aspirations that went far beyond the dark days of adult divorce, and the continual muted mutterings of the rosary by a ferocious grandmother, brought to me the greatest joy I ever experienced. Through this personal connection, I had my first real encounter with classical music. My pleasure, as I dug ever deeper to articulate tenderness and fragility and to infuse those notes below middle C with my own spiritual breath grew with hers. She didn't need to say anything. I felt it and responded. I looked at her and flew. She took me somewhere else: to a place unimagined and in the doing, gave me the greatest gift I have ever had. In those moments I was transformed; I was in another place and anything was possible. I learned about me, I saw what I could be and I learned about those rare transactions between people which involve all but the use of speech. That learning gave me a life of my own, distinct from the suffocating convent classrooms around us; it distanced the loneliness and terrors of my own home life; it formed an inner voice which has not only sustained me throughout my life but has helped me to challenge and to forge and to reconfigure.

All of this, a new strict code, a grammar system and a language of music through which I could find space and distance; speak emotion, find my own depth, make unspoken connections and create intimacy with others, often through playing music together, was challenging and thrilling. The techniques and musical conventions teased me as I struggled to grasp and master them; yet when I learned the how, I was overwhelmed by possibility and great joy. My secret world of finding a book about the concerto, reading the poetry of Matthew Arnold, the prose of Joseph Conrad; of discovering the Beethoven Violin Concerto, a Mozart opera... Don Giovanni, my first; Puccini's *Madame Butterfly* a few days later, performed by Scottish Opera; or of gazing at the grace of Degas ballerinas, the outrageousness of Lautrec posters; this was not something I would readily admit to or share. It was as raw as any of my first awareness of sexuality and arousal.

Much of this reflection, these fluctuations and this process of making my own decisions were private and because of this, they led to separation from my environment together with a degree of isolation from those I met in my day to day life at school, for I knew that this was a unique and personal experience. I was beginning more and more, to rely on the truth of my own instinct and feelings in response to what I observed around me.

Walking With and Losing Grandma

BY 1956 WE had moved into the new house my grandmother had bought in Bruntsfield, after a short spell living with my uncle and family in Morningside. This was when Grandma bought The Copper Kettle café which was to be the main focus of life for me and my family for many years to come. Our changed situation, my father no longer present but hovering in the shadows of my mother's and grandmother's consciousness, often consuming my mother with anguish for she became very black (in mood and appearance) and thin – meant that I then settled gratefully into my grandmother's bed.

Trying not to intrude into the life of my mother or the conversations between my grandmother and her son, was always a challenge. But my asthma meant that I could not help being ill often, which was thoroughly disruptive. It created a major upheaval. Kind Dr Shearer had to be called in and the day had to be organised around his arrival. Sometimes Dr McLaren would come instead. His smile was kindly too, but his rimless glasses and his quizzical expression made me shy. Each bout of asthma required perhaps three visits; I had to be confined to bed and given pills at regular intervals, and I didn't ever want anything to eat which horrified my grandmother for whom food spelt health. She would promise me five shillings for every cup of hot milk I drank. Milk then came to be associated with the smell of my leather schoolbag and with my grandmother's large warm bed and brightly lit bedroom where I drank saucerfuls in order to earn enough to buy a Matchbox car, a silver handgun like that of the Lone Ranger, a new book about the planets or the universe; another reason, maybe, for my variable relationship with milk. The unlikely gift of illness brought hours of uninterrupted glorious reading: history books about the Magna Carta and the Tudors; a brother and sister in the Highlands; the serialised magazine, *Knowledge*. The other benefit was the effect of ephedrine as medication. It quickened my heartbeat and caused me to be sleepless and loquacious. So we would lie side by side in the early hours, Grandma and I, she often facing the window, her back to me, rosary in hand, and I would chatter. These were the only times I spoke at length, when I had the full attention of an adult and I began to enjoy being listened to.

At school, as a young child, I was known to be quiet, saying nothing and constantly watchful. I had few, actually for some years, I had no friends. The children having 'cold lunches' were supervised in the Primary Two classroom by one of the nuns. After a spell, we were allowed outside to play. Those hours are almost too painful to recall. I was heavy with the unwelcome bulk of my own brooding presence, while all around me there was fun and chatter. But in those intimate waking hours, I had Grandma to myself and we talked as at no other time. She recited her mantras and curses and I gave voice. She prayed to all the Madonnas she believed in, for she was convinced that there were as many Virgin Marys as there were representations of her; she spoke of her life in Viticuso, of her courtship, of the unsuitable, discarded Tony, and Emilio who pursued her and would not give up. Her voice was still sweet in her seventies and she used to sing a little ditty that brought sunshine and the carefree days of her youth into that Edinburgh bedroom; a song that I can still almost remember '*com'è bello far l'amore, la domenica mattina… chi a letto a riposar'*, how wonderful to make love on a Sunday morning. She did then have her moments; and the specialness of Sunday in rural Italy… Mass, *l'aperitivo*, the gatherings of family for lunch, all of this I love to observe even when I am in Italy today.

Grandma's roots were in Viticuso, and although I have happy photographs of her with her sisters Zi' Martell' and Zi' Mink' and cousin Nicandro in Viticuso, I have no memory of her leaving for Italy in the fifties or later. Whether this was because of the unsettled situation in both countries after the war or because she felt the need to take care of me, I do not know. I do remember though, the joy with which she greeted the early morning, standing at the window of our ground floor flat. And as she looked out at Bruntsfield Links, The Copper Kettle café beyond, in her mind I know she saw Viticuso, the Apennines, the fields where her people toiled and the small home she had shared with my grandfather and their hens. They had married in 1911 and left for Scotland two years later. I am convinced that for my grandmother at least, marriage was a functional matter. Scotland must have been the plan, the courtship strategy, the 'better life'. Those morning visits to that window, her eye on the Bruntsfield Links and the potato fields of Lazio, a memory, *'Chill' beglie padan' re' Viticus'*, as she would say, were a coming to terms; the construction of a narrative for the events of her life in Scotland and the sum of her years. Her language was of journey and gratitude, despite the war and the loss of my grandfather. 'This country has been good to me', she would say. But in reality, her life was what she herself had made it, for she was an initiator, never standing still, skilful at integrating into Scottish life and winning hearts and admiration. Whatever she truly thought, I believe she never shared; her persona, always a willing one in that seductive Italian way, but dignified nonetheless, and refined. She had indeed 'mixed with her betters' and *'fatt' la spes'*, learned their ways. That example of aspiring, striving, moving, positioning and learning from others was a model for my own life journey. It was never about status but it was about leading rather than being led; being at the top. Winning.

She liked a gamble, though she couldn't read. She got help to do the football pools; and she had a sense not only of destiny but a belief in randomness, in luck. One of her intriguing skills was to read teacups. There were two main themes to these readings: one was prosperity, usually symbolised by a tree; the other was disaster... or death. There were other things... a stranger, a birth, a journey, a letter. Ernestina, young and fresh from Viticuso and eager for her own better future, used to listen attentively; and we would sit, the three of us, coven style, at the table in the kitchen recess, Ernestina and I watching Grandma's turning of cups, amazed.

I also have very happy memories of listening to a nightly exchange of ghost stories and spirit world tales between Grandma and Ernestina. I would be tucked up in bed beside Grandma and Ernestina would sit at the end of it, telling stories about apparitions on the road to Venafro or through the mountains to Cervaro; of snakes hypnotising breastfeeding mothers, taking the milk whilst soothing the baby with a tail. Folklore and superstition were a strong feature of the culture I grew up with. Between Grandma and Ernestina, the fireside telling of tales, a gathering of neighbours in the harsh cold of winter deep in the Apennines was recreated every night in a Bruntsfield flat. I was wide-eyed.

I grew up too in the care of a woman, who claimed she saw my grandfather standing in the hallway behind her on the afternoon of the morning he was drowned. As she was dressing to go out that morning, she looked in her long mirror, and there he was, she said, outside the bedroom, smiling in at her. Later on that day and on the many subsequent days of travels in a taxi from Edinburgh to the War Office in

Glasgow to find out if her husband had survived the sinking (some more fortunate families had already had good news) she heard him whistling behind her all the way; and this was also the woman who years later, when I was about twelve years old, went for her usual afternoon nap one day and woke up telling us that she had dreamt her brother Gelardin' in Canada had died: 'S'a mort' Gelardin'. It was then that Rico handed her an unopened black-bordered airmail letter on the thin paper of the time, which had arrived at his house and not ours. Her antidote was pragmatic and undramatic. Tears streaming, she methodically fried two fillets of lemon sole, placed them on a plate, an egg on top, and continuing to wipe her eyes, ate with gusto in front of my bewildered uncle, Ernestina and me. It was important, she said, 'pe' mantene' la salud, to keep your strength up.

First Confession, for a Roman Catholic, is an important landmark. This coming of age for me was to take place at school. I woke up with the early morning sun filling the bedroom and a sense of something different. Grandma was lying back, making strange sounds which weren't words. She got up and went through to my mother, and I could hear her trying to speak. I don't know what experience my mother had of these things, but she knew enough to call a doctor and my uncle. There were no lasting effects from that stroke but it was a signal of another change in the family.

As a countrywoman, Grandma was pragmatic about her death, for which she had made careful preparations. A favourite phrase of hers was 'quann' me mor' I', when I die, and this would lead to another new phase in her evolving plan. I have to admit that I have subconsciously taken to that same habit wth my own daughters, having recently walked them around the files and cupboards of my flat. The first sign of this preparing was her constant, diurnal and nocturnal, repetition of the rosary; she was always muttering, rosary beads were always in her hand. She would make her slowing progress down Greenhill Gardens to St Peter's RC Church for confession on a Saturday evening and early Mass on a Sunday. In our outings in Rico's car, there would be frequent trips on the way home (if I wasn't being annoyingly sick) to the cemetery at Mount Vernon while she decided which, not one, but six lairs, she would buy, for she clearly wanted a Rossi family mausoleum. During the days when I was in bed unwell and reading usually, I tried not to see the enormous statue of the Sacred Heart on Grandma's dressing table and the altar there, complete with candles and a standing crucifix. The bottom drawer of this piece of furniture was for the clothes she wanted to be laid out in, mainly white, delicate underwear. The undertaker would do the rest. In addition, there were two long candles and a bottle of Holy Water, brought from Lourdes, which she sometimes drank herself, or gave me to drink when I had a particularly bad asthma attack. These were to be placed beside her in her coffin. Not long before she died, she bought a set of receptacles for the oils and water used by the priest for the Last Rites, now referred to as the Sacrament of Healing. She was both thorough and realistic.

I was fourteen years old when Grandma died. I will never forget those hours of preparedness and of alertness for something I didn't fully understand. It was the first time death had entered my life. For some reason I went into Grandma's bedroom where my mother was sitting watching. Gigi, our distressed dog, had been banished earlier. He had cannily made his way to Grandma's bed and in what seemed a final farewell, had licked her hand. I noticed something strange about her left eye, a fixed glassy stare. I alerted my mother who immediately stood up and rushed over and tried to move her. We both stood watching as Grandma drew her last long breath. This left a very big impression on me. But what can haunt me still, is the sound of what I was told was 'the death rattle', which dominated the whole house for those interminable hours before she finally gave in. For she was stout-hearted and strong. Most of all, I remember the wood of the coffin, the satin lining, the hardness of her stone-cold skin, the surprising smallness of her and the unaccustomed expression of repose on her face. She was not the person I had known and loved. The greatness and glory of her, the power of her had departed, leaving behind only the feeble frame that contained and articulated them. I still see and smell those church candles in the room that was her bedroom and later became mine; the sickly scent of funeral wreaths covering most of the floor space in our house. To this day, I will not buy a wreath nor I would not allow them in my house when my mother died.

I have been very affected by death and my own especially has been a lurking presence every day of my life. The reality that it is, nods to me each morning and night and frequently backs me into a corner forcing me to look hard at it; unexpectedly and unprompted. It is a presence that watches me all the time; knows the when and the how, while I remain disturbed that I do not and will never know. On a whim, it will one day show itself in all its grim glory, it will choose its time and I will say to its face, 'Ah, you're here.'

The family had gathered in the hours before Grandma's death, dressed in black, and they paced the floor of the room next door to Grandma's bedroom as they waited for the end. For once, I do not remember drama of any kind; only dignity. Soon after, the house filled with people. The parish priest arrived and continued to come and go throughout the period between the death and the funeral. Some nuns from my school followed. Men came with whisky; shopkeepers, sellers of wafers and cones, makers of pasta, of ice cream and of fudge; café and restaurant owners, car dealers and grocers; the God-fearing and the womanisers, the drinkers, the shady; the Padre Pio, the Lourdes and the Fatima fanatics;

the pallid and the bronzed; the swaggerers, the humble and the earnest. There were open shirts, bow-ties, waistcoats, sparkle and velvet; shoes of crocodile, of patent leather and of cool suede; the bald, the Brylcreemed, the backslappers and the blessed; the fragrant, the fresh, the bearded and moustached; the overdone, the overbearing, the mighty and the slight; those who wept and those whose large laughter filled the house. Parked outside... the big red Zaccardelli and Cervi truck, the Coletta-owned Daimler, the modest Morrises and Fords, the Jaguars and a variety of ice cream vans; each an indicator of rank and fortune: these were the Edinburgh Italians of the sixties.

There were a few old ladies, dressed all in black, friends of Grandma's, women who had shared the stuff and twists of history and rooting in a strange new world, their men gone. Some asked my dead grandmother to pass on messages; to say hello; all of them spent minutes by the coffin praying in Italian, moving rosary beads about. One still beautiful, gentle old woman in black, wearing a veiled hat, asked for time on her own with my grandmother. But her heartbreaking pleas for Grandma to tell her husband, that 'she was sorry' for her adultery could be heard in the next room.

Such was the intimacy of the Italian community that the old way of visiting the house of the bereaved was customary even in Scotland among second and third generation Italians. There was no delay. Within the hour a queue formed at the door and down the street. The house became a thoroughfare. I moved around it and through it, tasked to serve the guests, but mainly watching. Strangely, I did not cry once. Nor did I cry in the months that followed. Subdued, I wore black as bid, modulating to grey later, as was the norm in our community.

It was traditional for guests to take over the house, relation or not; to look after the children, answer the telephone and the doorbell, wash dirty dishes or clothes, deal with the detritus from the death; principally to bring food and drink, cook and serve the mourners and the bereaved family. For the thinking was, it was important to maintain strength at a time of shock and loss. Equally, the bereaved would neither think of eating or have any interest in preparing food. It was also customary for two rooms to be used for the purpose: one room where the body was laid out and where each visitor was expected to view, kiss, take their final leave of the dead person; and another for social interaction. This practice could be awkward for the squeamish, the nervous or those who felt no sense of loss at the death, for one would be closely observed and most especially if there had been any difficulty or issue between the person gone and the person standing at the coffin. Children were often included in the rituals. They were not spared any of the physical processes or the emotion. My presence at all of it was not so very unusual. Any prayers were confined to the room with the body while the other room was a room of recovery, healing and distraction. It was also the room where food and drink, though never tea, were to be had. Tears were shed in both and by most, however they felt, for Italians cry in the presence of strong emotion; and people often went between the two rooms.

When I was a student at university, the father of a close friend of mine died in tragic circumstances. I immediately went to visit him and expecting a crowd, I blundered in with a tray of pasta and a bottle of Talisker whisky. I found my friend and his wife sitting quietly at home in lone privacy. I was as astonished by that as they were by my sudden, unbidden arrival. As a reaction to this, when the father of a good friend died, despite my strong impulse to be with her, I maintained a respectful distance, seeing her only as we filed out of the church: 'Where have you been?' she asked. Difficulty in responding appropriately to death is not limited to my Scottish experience. I had a similar embarrassment in

France when the father of our host, Patrick, died suddenly. Having taken Patrick to catch the first plane to Paris, I shopped for a banquet and cooked a meal of seafood for his wife and children, which I realised later must have looked like a celebration.

At these Scottish-Italian gatherings in those post-war years, at the funerals, weddings and christenings, the language spoken was, perhaps surprisingly, generally English intoned in a way that was more country Italian than Scottish; pronounced in the manner of a resident of the Grassmarket, Newhaven or Leith. Whether this adoption of English was a natural development or an effect of the war, of internment and therefore a deliberate attempt to disguise ethnic difference, whether it was a new demographic, a sign of natural integration, or quite simply the result of a Scottish education, it is hard to say. The dialect was but a tracing, a humorous sprinkling, a means of emphasis. It was easier to curse or utter expletives using the rough language of intimacy and cradle. And it was all the more powerful when interspersed with English. Sometimes to use the dialect is a necessity, there being nothing in the English language appropriate to what is required. Furthermore, the dialect also serves as a means of connection, an acknowledgement of roots, blood and ancestry: *È cumpá* is a greeting between fellow Italians; *va coll' la lun'*, literally, she changes with the moon or she/he is unpredictable; *cott' pe n'om*, she is hot for a man, wants to get laid; *schivos*, disgusting just doesn't render it at all! And my favourite, *nun ce ver cchiù' pe' la fam'*, I'm so hungry I've gone blind! Finding the right phrase works the other way too. That famous *com'e va gle business?*, how's business?; *tre pund'*, three pounds. English words did then also become absorbed into the Italian of the community. Then there is the linguistic mix of 'I *schiv* that', that makes me sick.

There are some interesting studies on the links between

language and identity; the fluidity of identity or identities and what it is that we really share when we are in conversation. These propositions are all the more interesting when applied to a community in transition, where the languages used represent markers of both a cultural identity and an identity aspired to. What I know to be the case then is that, unlike subsequent Italian immigration to Scotland, in the fifties for example, when people were more literate through their exposure to the media, speaking Italian as their main language and not dialect, the post-war generation of Italians, my mother's generation, living in Scotland could speak very little dialect. Though having been brought up with it they understood it completely. What is more, they had very little Italian if at all, something that surprises Scottish friends. I have been embarrassed many times by the attempts of my mother, my uncle and family in Italy or when speaking to Italians from Italy, at converting their limited *laziale* language, with all its truncations, rich consonantal texture, its archaisms of vocabulary that is the character of it, for it is sadly a dying language into something equating the elegant flow of Italian.

The prudishness of my own generation in relation to our Italian heritage, mirroring a reluctance among educated Italians in Italy to acknowledge or even reply in a dialect we both have, is now, in a more recent valuing of Italians and all things Italian maybe changing, certainly in the Scotland I live in. Possibly for Italians living in Italy it is too soon to look back and own roots. A united Italy is still a recent event and there is an immense cultural and economic dichotomy between the prosperity, sophistication and liberalism of the North and the mores, norms and values of the rural South. A certain covering of one's tracks is maybe still required. In Scotland, by comparison, roots are valued and the more diverse the better. The culture and dialects that we inherited from our immigrant families are increasingly becoming the stuff of academia, life stories and research. Italian is now synonymous with flair and creativity. There is a respect for our enterprise and endeavour and a recognition of the impact we have had on the fabric and institutions of this country. Our imprint is to be found in every profession and area of Scottish life, in almost every town, hamlet and city. We now find ourselves trumpeting a colourful, glorious tradition, one to be envied. No longer downtrodden, fearful, hopeful and apologetic, we see pizzerías, panettone, Illy coffee and Gaggia coffee machines, as a sign of quality. Replacing the standard vanilla of our early years of Italian ices, sold from barrows and vans, there is a gelato industry. Across Europe, in Greece, Spain, France and beyond, flavoured ice cream of every description can be had, the most intriguing being still for me, apple crumble and naughty *zabaglione*.

I was very fortunate to have the opportunity to speak and understand that beautiful laziale dialect. That *viticusar* language of fun and laughter, of life at its most basic, of a shared awareness of the challenges of life and a wisdom about the ways of human nature. I never spoke it with my mother nor she with me, but in Ernestina's last days, I remember sitting with her in the bay window of her lounge, softened by the green of the old trees outside, laughing freely over tea and talking *viticusar* in a way that we had not for years, in the language of her beginning here in Scotland and my childhood.

In my late teens, somewhat reluctantly, in order to qualify for entrance to a degree in languages at Edinburgh University, I learned Italian in three months and I lived in Florence for five. I have fluency, but my Italian never has quite the authenticity and naturalness of the language of my home.

Maria Coletta: 1888 to 1964

Sometimes you sang to me
an old Italian song
from the potato fields and the crumbled stonework
of that time and that place
where your jug sat proud upon your head
as you walked,
and the dough was warming
by a fireside where spirit stories hung
and love was shy;
and it was a song from sunshine
on the soft ground of valleys, embroidery and lacework,
from Sunday bells, a saint's shrine
the Septembers of children, chestnuts,
the masquerades of festival;
and maybe a chicken taken unaware
for the stone bench you called a table.

And when you sang there was the girl on your lips
for you always had slim ankles.

Terra Straniera: An Education

A COLD MORNING in November and I do not want to get out of the narrow bed in a heavy-oaked Victorian room which was probably not intended to be a dormitory for three adolescent girls. I am younger than my roommates and they whisper stories every night, when the lights have been switched off, about a young, blond-haired fisherman in St Abbs called Aly and a shy boy in Perthshire. It is six am. I pick up the plastic jug on my locker and head to the area where the taps are located. Other boarders are yawning, slopping and mumbling early morning exchanges. I haven't been a boarding pupil for very long at St Margaret's Convent, though I am now fourteen years old and have been at the school since the age of five. I do not want to board but maybe it might be better than being at home. I always wear grey clothes because I am 'in mourning', and my mother tells me that I now have to be a boarder because she needs to be in the shop. There had been little discussion about this plan. All I remember is my aunt from Blackpool's visit, the rush to hand-sew all the labels with my name onto my clothes, and the sudden appearance of a Stewart tartan rug and a very large blue trunk. The strange thing about this is that I am to be a full-time boarder not a weekly boarder, which means I am not to return home until the school holidays, although my school is a five or ten minute walk from our shop.

Conscious of the ease between those around me and feeling

no comfort or sense of belonging myself, I unobtrusively brush my teeth without looking up from the sink and return to my sleeping area with my jug full of warm water. I pull the curtains around my bed... we are clear that only when we are washing and dressing or when we are ill should these curtains be closed. The entire room must be visible at one sweep to whoever opens the door. There is usually only one visit, around ten o'clock. The older girls take the visit as a signal that they are now free to talk and they wait in silence for it, sometimes reading by torchlight under the bedclothes, listening out for the swish and click of the large rosary beads hanging down the length of the nun's habit that announces the approach of Mother Enda or Mother Celsius. It is rare for Mother Martina to put in an appearance. She has her own room on the ground floor of the building, which is both the Primary School and a boarding house. In the corridor on the other side of the very large mirror that separates her bedroom from the kitchen and utility area, there is a serving hatch from which each break time sweets are sold. The other two nuns sleep by the door of the large dormitories where the younger girls are. Mother Martina herself did once appear in the middle of one night when a large number of us had gathered for midnight feasting on cream eggs, crisps and a large quantity of chocolate. We had planned this tryst for days, squirrelling food from the serving area in the large dining room into napkins, bags and whatever was to hand. I had also been commissioned to ask for what I could from my mother's shop. It was the drama of the vision that night that I remember, the large blackness of her suddenly filling the doorway, catching us unawares, the loosely fastened white collar at her throat, the bluish redness of her usually pink fleshy cheeks, the thunderous silence of her as we wordlessly tiptoed out through the door she held open and oddly, the lack of any kind of repercussion.

I sponge and dry myself on the thin towel which is more

like a dish towel and get dressed in my navy uniform... in my collared wool jumper and tie with purple and white stripes on navy. This is winter garb. In summer we wear blue and white striped dresses gathered below the waistband, a blazer and a straw hat. One felt for the full-figured girls. I make my bed, draw back the screen and take my jug to the sinks to empty and rinse it and then return it to my bedside locker. I make my way to the table on the landing. There is one large bathroom on the upper floor of this building which we can only use with permission, once a week for a bath and twice a week for hair washing. This bathroom is where the nuns perform their daily ablutions, which must take place before we in the dormitories are on the move, because I never saw a nun in nightwear. There is a black plastic Macintosh hanging behind the door, so that the nuns and presumably we too can maintain our modesty while bathing and to protect us from any impure thoughts we might have at the sight of our own nakedness. There was one occasion when my friend Heather and I decided to break the rules and wash our hair together without asking. We were spotted just as we made to close the door and when I looked through the keyhole, one dark eye on the other side of it looked back at me.

This landing is where we gather to say the rosary together each night in October, which is the month of the Holy Rosary, and then, berets on, metal school badge to the front, tassels for the élite school hockey team, down the imposing staircase we go and in twos, along a dark and silent Whitehouse Loan at six forty am; we cross the road to the big school and into the stark, simple chapel which brings you naturally to your knees and invites stillness. There is a one-bar electric fire on the second step of the altar for the priest, and we kneel one behind the other, upright, facing the front, shivering in the ornate wooden structure called a stall, where each individual has their space and the seat can be lowered for sitting to face those in the opposite row. It is so cold that my fingers and feet are numb and when I breathe I create a cloud of mist in the air.

There is a set seating order in this extraordinarily beautiful little chapel. The girls are centrally placed while the nuns have their own allocated spaces in taller, more spacious stalls around the sides and at the back. The Reverend Mother, Sister Raphael (whom my grandmother knew well), the religious leader of the community of Ursulines of Jesus, a French order, sits just inside the wooden archway to the left. The Headmistress, Mother John, sits next to her. Despite the close-eyed supervision and formality of morning Mass, which is unsung every day except Sundays and Feast Days (when there is High or sung Mass) and starts at 7am each day and which we are obliged to attend at least twice weekly, there were a few noteworthy incidents. Of these there was the time that Gip, the school mongrel, who was totally feral, leapt onto the altar and started to bark menacingly at reedy Father McPhillips as he and we stumbled our way through the *Kyrie Eleison*. The other was when, while carrying the chalice to the altar, he accidentally tripped on the wire of the heater and fell flat causing a gasp from the nuns and a rush through the altar rails to check if he was still with us (but I suspect not from them all and certainly not from the more libertarian of them, who were open-minded enough to feel they could laugh at least inwardly). While we felt able to laugh at the first incident, since there was no implied disrespect to God's messenger, man or dog, our giggles certainly had to be stifled at the second. This in itself, because of its illegitimacy, heightened the hysteria, causing seats to creak and bringing forth odd noises including coughing and snorting, objects to be dropped.

The entire Mass was said in Latin and we responded using a Missal as a prompt, though by this stage I knew the Latin by heart. Priests at that time celebrated Mass with their backs to the worshippers. Also the ruling then was that nothing except water could be taken from midnight before communion was taken. It was the Vatican Council begun in 1962, led by Pope John XXIII, that changed these practices. Vatican Two was a bold step towards modernising the Catholic Church. I had not eaten or drunk anything since supper at six thirty the previous evening because I intended to take communion and, for the first and only time in my life, I had the sensation of fainting. I did not actually lose consciousness but I lost immediate contact with the scene around me as I travelled at speed through a dark tunnel, a strong wind on my face. It was a struggle to remain connected with where I was; however after sitting down for a few moments I recovered enough to be able to kneel again and speak the required words.

Another unusual incident occurred towards the end of my school years which was memorable. Rather than a physical sensation, this was a unique spiritual experience, somewhat akin to a kind of enlightenment. As I sat at the back of the chapel sometime in the late afternoon, after the Benediction rite and the host was 'exposed' or visible for veneration and prayer, there was a heavy silence. I gazed upwards towards the monstrance containing the consecrated host, and through the incense I had a strong sense of glimpsing divinity, the Almighty and almost touching something just out of my reach.

The chapel always moved me to a place of stillness and when I eventually and conclusively dismissed Catholicism and indeed an all-loving God in my early thirties, suddenly realising that I was praying to a void, it was not the lack of a Presence, but that stillness, of space and of gathering myself to myself that I missed; a reconciling with my own truth. Before that, a few lapses apart, I had been a devout Catholic. I believed and argued with sincerity and all my intellectual energy, using my fairly solid grasp of the New Testament. In my late teens and then again in my mid twenties I felt drawn to the life of a religious, to the ascetic and discipline of Holy Orders. I saw myself leading a life of prayer, of Gregorian chant and a mix of Teilhard de Chardin and Michel Quoist:

Lord, why did you tell me to love all men, my brothers? I have tried, but I come back to you, frightened... Lord, I was so peaceful at home, I was so comfortably settled. It was well furnished, and I felt cozy. I was alone, I was at peace. Sheltered from the wind, the rain, the mud. I would have stayed unsullied in my ivory tower. But, Lord, you have discovered a breach in my defences, You have forced me to open my door, Like a squall of rain in the face, the cry of men has awakened me; Like a gale of wind a friendship has shaken me, As a ray of light slips in unnoticed, your grace has stirred me... and, rashly enough, I left my door ajar. Now, Lord, I am lost! Outside men were lying in wait for me. I did not know they were so near; in this house, in this street, in this office; my neighbour, my colleague, my friend.

(Quoist, *Prayers of Life*)

While I have put both religion and these aspects of it to one side at certain periods of my life, luxuriating at times in materialism and a good measure of hedonism, which was fun and which I enjoyed, they are nonetheless central to who I deeply am; in theological and philosophical debate, I seek a faith which eludes me. It is the asceticism of camping, rather than the sport of it, the privations, the simplicity and confrontation with solid fundamentals which are home to me. I am moved by French Gothic and Romanesque churches because of their architectural simplicity and balance of light and stone. The spareness and bare bones of Bach and fugue... intricacies woven around one clean tune give me clarity; I am most happy when alone amidst the whiteness of the skies and beaches in the Hebrides. I embrace my simple room on the Buddhist centre of Holy Isle with only a bed, a chair and a writing desk. Travelling around Scotland, its hostels, on the buses or on my bike, in my sixties and with no plan, unencumbered, makes me open and receptive to all around me. My greatest joy ever is to be seated as close as possible to the platform in a concert hall, when my breath becomes the music, the music my breath, and fine chorales, mighty choruses leave me limp, choking at the enormity and tearful at the tenderness.

At St Margaret's I felt bewildered at my new status of boarder, having to engage continually with an unfamiliar community of girls, forced to make decisions without reference to anyone else. Yet for the first time in my life, I felt the power of choice and the exhilaration of freedom. I saw opportunity and I slowly began to realise that this was a start. I was liberated. My behaviour, my attachments could be dictated only by my own responses. If I felt left out, sad, indignant, I did something about it. I could act on my excitement, respond generously to feeling valued, liked or sought-after. I was able to both keep and reject aspects of my old life, my Italian life. I could act on the natural and what was comfortable. This is what would define me. So, my boarding school years from the age of fourteen to seventeen marked the beginning of my exit from an Italian background into a new way of thinking, and my first self-making; building on my upbringing, redefining, reducing, denying it and moving in another direction completely. Above all, I wanted to dismiss the ways, the self-limiting and determining precepts of my Italian home and the small, uninventive aspirations of those I grew up with.

I found, for instance, that by way of contrast with that anxiety-provoking house of excess, tension, and unschooled behaviour, what I took to as a boarder was the daily routine; the planned; the structure, the calm, the order and discipline.

I found this reliability offered security... the study hours after supper, the allotted time for relaxation and games after teaching had finished, the set times for eating meals, the quiet, subdued voices, the respectful exchanges even in fierce disagreement, and most of all the importance given to school work, manners, culture and learning. Here there was no television, no shop to dominate, no interruption, no traffic of hungry family, no after-hours *frittata,* no undercurrents; only books, music, ideas, uproarious fun and thoughtful conversation. My grades improved. I liked the feeling of being part of a special group among the day girls, the familiarity with the teaching nuns, and the pointers to poets, Masefield, Manley Hopkins, Rossetti, religious writing, classical music and art that entered those discussions. It was here early on that I found Antoine de Saint-Exupéry, *Terre des Hommes, Vol de Nuit* and of course *Le Petit Prince,* and I asked myself the big questions. What is it that the heart can know?

Unlike anyone in previous generations on either side of my family, Italian or Scottish, I made the decision to go to university. Before I was a boarder, I had never even encountered the word 'university'. I grew to see myself as a serious and able student with a university education as my goal. To continue to learn and study and the way of life and refinement it brought, was what I wanted for myself. My mother had resisted relentless pressure from Rico to put me behind a shop counter. She later told me that a teacher from my earliest time in primary school had told her that I had that potential, but the word was never mentioned to me. My cousins all struggled at school and became ultimately involved in the family business. But my mother's determination to do whatever she could to allow me to learn and develop, her wishes counter to family advice and some pressure, must have been because of that conversation. It may have been a reaction to her unsuccessful bid to flee the family, because her main advice to me was to ensure that whatever I chose to do in life, it must guarantee my ability to live independently of anyone else.

My experience of being a boarder was in sharp contrast to the lives of my cousins. In each branch of my family, in Loanhead, Morningside, Blackpool and Huddersfield, the shop was a way of living. Shop opening, which sometimes extended until the small hours, and the continual requirements of the business (for there were no holiday closures or lunch breaks), regular stock delivery and ordering, dashes to the local wholesaler or 'cash and carry', trips to the bank or worse, the bank manager, and keeping a vigilant eye on the blessed till, dictated when meals were taken, who worked when and even how free time was spent; for an urgent need for sugar, piece of linoleum or picture hooks could arise without warning. It was rare if ever, maybe for a few hours on Christmas Day, for the entire family to be together. This was especially true in my own case because it was only my mother who was the provider and almost all the living was in the shop. But even in the other family homes, where men saw to the business and wives kept house, everyone in the family, including wives and each of my cousins still at school and at an early age, helped or did a shift in the shop. In the best of Italian homes there was an acknowledgement of the importance of academic qualifications, but while the words were spoken, that was not the prime concern and the time allowed for study and homework was in practice secondary to the practicalities of making a living or for girls, running the home. School work was quickly disposed of in order to attend to the real business of the smooth running of the household and the fount of all family resources.

In this environment there was little opportunity for any kind of intellectual growth or social or cultural development. Our Scottish peers had so much more freedom to mix and befriend, to read, take up an instrument or develop an interest of their own. In the Rossi home of my closest cousins, the boys were encouraged into sport as a relaxation from the drudgery of ice cream making and filling pails of half-blanched chips and stacking the cigarettes in the right order on the shelves; but I cannot think of an equivalent distraction for the girls, though a little shopping, makeup and clothes were to some extent tolerated. Pursuits that were neither utilitarian nor essential for day-to-day living were not easily accessible, and the young Italians were and possibly many still are, expected to work at the end of the school day or weekends while their Scottish equivalents attend theatre workshops or played hockey on Saturdays. As for friends and meeting the opposite sex, these constraints meant that the pool for choosing was a small one. Socialising and opportunities for dating were often limited. A cousin might be a best friend or even a love interest leading in some cases to marriage. Not only were Italian families generally closed off from mainstream Scottish society (some remain so), but the experience of the young of the Italian community was so different that their currency with Scots of similar age was minimal.

To aim for university was a defining aspiration. My choice of how to spend my free time, my choice of friends and my appearance, very different from that of my cousins, represented the beginning of a distancing I needed and wanted. This has only deepened over the years, for we no longer have a common language or terms of reference. I became someone my family could never encompass; unusual, 'brainy' and certainly not one of them.

My journey through the school years was not smooth. My position in class (we were placed at the end of each academic year), varied from thirty second out of thirty-five pupils to third in the class. My academic performance and my study habits were erratic partly because I was looking for some steady direction – there was no home steer; partly because of my family background and the business/Italian environment;

and partly too because I could be easily distracted and was often unwell. There was simply my mother's commitment, through providing for me, and my own will and mental resources which sometimes failed. Nevertheless, it was quite obvious from my first year and certainly by my third year in secondary school, that I would study languages. So having declared my post-school intentions to my teachers, my status now greatly enhanced, I was singled out in my sixth year and given additional tuition to prepare me. I was given extra books to read in my own time and introduced to Sartre, Beaumarchais, Racine and Corneille as part of the A level syllabus.

My piano playing had also moved on very rapidly. I had musical talent. Indeed my second-hardest life decision was whether I should keep with the plan to choose a career in education or continue with music. No longer at home in the evenings or after school, I was able to play the piano for as long as I wanted, work endlessly at scales, outing the middle voice in counterpoint and not having to be mindful of the family in the kitchen wanting to switch on *Coronation Street* in the sitting room where the piano was. The school pianos were mainly well tuned. There were a number to choose from, although I liked the upright in the blue room best when I wanted privacy. The best instrument was the fine grand in the school hall. And it was here that for the first time, those around me wanted and asked to hear me play; that I had the appreciation and attention of other people; especially when I knocked out Jolson's 'Rock a Bye' after supper. In four short years, I transited from beginning to learn the piano to being a Grade Eight pianist; playing the repertoire, playing for school assemblies, competitions and public events. I began to explore piano concertos bringing back piano scores from the library, attacking Beethoven, breathless with excitement. I started an after-school music appreciation club with my new-found confidence, I arranged a piece written for piano for the house choir and having previously been shy, silent and once even physically bullied, I conducted it with the entire school present. I became popular, looked up to by the younger girls. I relaxed. I finally had friends.

The Italian ways I had been separated from not through choice became increasingly distasteful. Supper here was eaten at six thirty. I was astonished at standard boiled eggs for dinner each Sunday night, and the scant fare generally. I had never eaten rissoles or fishcakes before, and bread and jam was a novelty. But I found that I quite enjoyed this diet, this way; and teatime-eating replacing dinner or *pranzo*. There was no denying that I bore some traces of Scottishness, for I took to these food practices eventually, but I remained half-Italian. I had been around Italians all my life. My heritage was undeniable. When I consider that time, my Italianism was evident in the thrill of performing, leading, grandstanding, being acknowledged, being the best; in initiating and venturing into new projects, in finding friends and sociability; in my ability to mimic and my easy flow of authentic French. With a lifestyle that I welcomed and the chance to enter the circle and have a strong role at the party, life as a boarder became some of the happiest years I had ever experienced. To this day, I remember that period of my life with great warmth.

One final image of the last day at school remains with me. I had been part of a close group in my sixth year. We had walked by the River Forth during exam months, crossing in that tiny little boat, sunbathed in that old suntrap down the slope under the Senior three classroom, made daisy chains in the school field during sports day, gone to discos organised for the Young Helpers of Lourdes, which the sixth year from a boys' private Catholic school also came to and where a few exchanged a first kiss. We had gathered laburnum from the trees in the school grounds to line the path for the passage of the Blessed Sacrament on Corpus Christi, and we had sung and harmonised a lot together. After the farewells, single file processions, music, speeches and the tears of the last school assembly in the main hall, six of us went into the chapel, knelt at the altar and solemnly sang *Veni Domine et Noli Tardare*, and then one by one exited by the main gate. That experience of boarding in St Margaret's Convent, the four years of it, was one of self-making. And it was I believe where I, the only one in my family, crossed the Italian/Scottish divide.

Mandolin Annie

can ye no haud me agane
an Ah'll coorie doon
frae they safe thighs o' yours
wi' the tang o'earth
an yer fingers rootin' about me
tae find a guid tune.
A'll be that close to yer hert,
hear yer songs i the makin'
aw wee that a am
a'll gie strength tae yer airm.

Spotlights

Glorious France: A Study in Self-Making

PARIS IN JUNE 1970; the end of my year in France as part of my degree course; a vibrant Matisse palette, his major exhibition in the Bibliothèque Nationale that year; a memorable conversation about artistry and possibility; then one single, defining moment. I looked out over the familiar, iconic landmarks of the city and up to industrial glass and steel high above, the sky a promising blue, a dawning... a new era beginning, all mine. I was finally ready to embrace it, free to inhabit and fashion it. This was my time and my life and I instantly resolved to live it. To remain in all the wonderful years ahead, coolly unhampered by the claustrophobic clamouring, entrapments of guilt, duty and even love; for love as I had experienced it had not been love of me. Never once in my childhood and adolescence had I felt loveable. All the beautiful words that people use for children had never been mine. I had been an ungainly, unbecoming load which my mother struggled to carry. She was seeking her own liberation, finally, after the death of her mother, when she was nearing her middle age.

Standing on that threshold in June 1970 in the Tuileries gardens, the fresh and the undiscovered around and before me, I felt light, aware of my own power and of my selfness, of my ability to be whoever I determined to be. I made up my mind to challenge norms rather than settle into them, to question and critique rather than to accept, to value the untried, to adopt an ideology of the contemporary, of ideas and trends in the making, of future in every aspect of life. That was the moment of my steely partition from the tired, crushing old order of family and friends; from a religion which offered no answers, safeguards or resolution; and from a past which I determined would not claim me. This was the time of the first appearance of responsibility to myself, cleansed of my history, unwritten and fully ready.

I met Marie-Cécile in the convent hostel where, on my arrival in France, I first found lodgings. It was 1969. She was studying Dentistry at the University of Montpellier. We eventually took a flat in the Montpellier suburbs, sharing with a childhood friend of hers from Millau, a small town in l'Aveyron in the Midi-Pyrénnées. My conversations with Marie-Cécile were mainly about the arts. Newly qualified that year with a diploma from the London College of Music as a sideline to my degree in Modern Languages, I traded my developing knowledge and my appetite for music of almost every kind, but especially for Beethoven, in return for her thoughts on and her increasing yearnings for fine art and becoming an artist herself. I shared with her that violin concerto, Beethoven's, as my first awakening to spiritual power, other than the power of any God or religion, such as Roman Catholicism with which I had grown up, and my realisation, my deep understanding that the arts can say most eloquently that which speech cannot. I had also begun to write poetry and had had some publishing success which she embellished with her great love of Lorca, and that took me in other directions.

During that year in Montpellier, frequently in Millau, for we visited her family there, regularly hitching lifts usually from long-distance lorry drivers, I was under Marie-Cécile's unyielding ever caring eye. Through her, close friend and mentor, and my frequent contact with her family, honest and warm, I learned for the first time harmony within family life and bonds created by the sustaining heartbeat of a loving mother who was a quiet, solid, reflective source of all nourishment for everyone in the household and anyone associated with it. Marie-Cécile's house was the home of jams, savoury puddings, forty-eight-hour beef stews and slow, stove-cooked game. For Madame, consistent in all things, was a magnificent cook as well as the driving force in the business of this family of jewellers and watchmakers. The clients respected her. Her husband and son, front of shop, followed her quiet, steady lead from the back room. She was fine-featured, refined in speech and manner, in all respects cultured, with a love of literature, and the gift of laughter.

I will never forget the engagement party of her younger son, Jacques. Her older son, Jean, was studying for the priesthood. After and between many courses of the finest food I had ever seen, and it has to be said that I have never been as heavy since that year in France, there were organised games, singing, storytelling and I learned there, the finest drinking songs which I sing to this day. But my main memory is of her wicked participation in a game which all the guests seemed to know well and which I have never seen since. The men were robbed of their socks and shoes and were made to sit trousers rolled up to the knee. Then, blindfolded, the women came into the room one by one, feeling their way down the line, to their husbands. Madame Froment set about the task energetically with all the experience of the seasoned lover of a rollickingly unpolished Frenchman from Northern France, the father of her children. As a woman from the luxuriant, green southern lands of pasture for ewes, flowers for honey bees, the thick, tarry tongue of Georges Brassens and the Auvergne, from a land of rosemary and the bluest of cheeses, in themselves a delicate science of density and moistness, she was, in those smiling moments, equally the natural, comfortable mother of four children and a deft woman who knew her man by touch.

The ample architect-built house, comfortable and sturdy amidst gardens of hanging vines, bougainvillea, bushes of lavender, thyme and bay was fuelled, resourced, preserved and presented by Marie-Cécile's mother. It was the home that her grown children, two at university and two in work, came back to, and a house for receiving close family friends. In contrast to my childhood experience, I saw there a place of order and seemly behaviour, a place of retreat and restoration, a source of physical energy and wellbeing. It was the combination of tranquility, of kindly, loving tolerance of eccentricities and human foibles, and of an environment where the land and nature were so central to life and the enjoyment of it, that made it so strengthening for those who lived there. I was surprised to find myself suddenly excited and joyous at the start of each of my days there. I was not Italian, not Scottish, but culturally open and growing. I did of course have an understanding of what I observed in the Froment home since it was other than Scottish, closer to the Italian ways I grew up with, but it was as if the elements of mine had been somehow reordered into one cohesive whole there; honed and refined into a purpose and an interaction between people that was altogether civil, thoughtful and sophisticated. As I exited the shower each day, groomed in a way that I had newly learned, as I embraced the rhythms and dynamics of a new language, collecting words, I felt that this was a truer me. As I set about my *bol* of coffee for breakfast, my *tartines au beurre,* country bread with butter, and *confiture aux abricots,* apricot jam, fruit from the garden and cooked in that wonderful house, I can easily say that I began to live my life, the one which I had been preparing for in my last years at school but without those constraints or impositions. Unmade and unfinished, I had come to this family with a need but not an intention to set my feet on good soil, which would hold me up and give me an identity that I could present to the world with the assurance and a congruence that I badly needed.

In the leaving of my mother at Waverley station in Edinburgh, I felt no sentimentality and only opportunity very close at hand. Walking in the footsteps of my grandmother, with her counsel in mind, I was learning from Marie-Cécile, not only about art, literature and philosophy, but also about the creative impulse, about reaching an understanding of the world which we inhabit and the potential of the arts not only to offer a perspective on what is but what will or could be. Marie-Cécile was relentless in her schooling of me and my French; permitting no aberrations of language, despairing at the slightest grammatical fault. She was amused at my Scottishness, my unpolished presentation; highly critical of my Italian ways, which to her were unruly. Speaking too loudly, flouting traffic regulations with my bicycle, shouting, these offended her sense of order and decorum. Through observation, through slowly seeing myself through her eyes, I began to understand my life as a continual piece of self-presentation. Interest in clothes and fashion, while often seen as superficial, I began to regard as having the potential to volunteer a unique personal commentary to the world about who we are. Presentation can suggest belonging, an intention, a hint of something unique to offer.

This was provincial France in the late sixties and Marie-Cécile was not alone in her disapproval of my unstylish garb. I was often made to feel uncomfortable in cafés and restaurants because of my blatantly ill-combined appearance and my noticeable lack of interest in it. There is a very old southern Italian saying *te trov alle ball e ter a ballà,* literally, when at the dance, you must dance, meaning fit in, do as others do, the old adage of Italian immigrants. And so with my French haircut, new rimless glasses, my pipe of Clan tobacco, my Gauloises Bleues, and my two Cacharel blouses, ill-afforded, having put the ugly old clothes I had arrived with into a trunk bound for Edinburgh, also at some expense, I created another identity and a currency. For whatever reason it came so easily. I was acquiring a taste for the outrageous on the one hand, an obsession with fashion on the other. Neither has ever left me. I enjoyed disrupting convention and expectations but also learned that it could only be done from a position of acceptability. Appearance was a marker of how well I fitted in. And I very much wanted to belong generally, and most especially in France.

An unwavering eye, like that of Marie-Cécile, creates a great deal of self-evaluation and introspection. Equally strong became my determination to taste and to explore the new and unknown; areas of knowledge and activity I knew nothing about, had no experience of. I enrolled at the music Conservatoire in Montpellier, longing to play a piano again and to be surrounded by the production of musical sound. I abandoned my classes at the Faculté des Lettres and went exploring my surroundings on my *motocyclette* instead. The day that I rolled over the handlebars while travelling downhill at speed has left some scars and provided my first experience of a French hospital. I lay on the beaches of Palavas, covered in olive oil in order to bronze my body more efficiently, reading sometimes aloud: Pagnol, Sagan, Hugo. I savoured a language that has always been for me, precise and compact; liquid, fruity and soft; words which roll and fill your mouth; words that make you drool. I bought the books of San Antonio and worked hard at acquiring French slang. I bought myself a Livre de Poche series on Physics, which I never understood. I developed an appreciation of French Gothic churches, elegant arches flying skywards, rose windows colouring paving stones and altar tables and I learned to spot Romanesque, squat, satisfyingly solid. I found a *Concise History of Art* in English in three volumes, which I took to Florence and studied attentively, learning by heart for instance, the differentiating features of Ionic, Corinthian and Doric columns of Ancient Greece and Rome. Then later, with no prior understanding or background in drama as an art form, I chose as an experiment Twentieth Century French Drama, the Absurd, Ionesco, Beckett, Anouilh, Genet, as my final Honours specialism, which turned out to be unwise and of which I have no recollection at all.

I did not attend to the matter of research for my final dissertation for my degree. In fact I sat up all one night before the final date for submission and both started and finished it, in a manner of speaking. Nor did I pay much heed to the translation assignments that arrived monthly from my university in Edinburgh. I returned them completed but disinterestedly, since my thoughts were elsewhere. I was distracted by this new life, by my new-found ability to be exhilarated, to feel that all and anything was within my reach. I started to write poetry in French, I took lessons in drawing, which I have no ability for. I deserted the Church for it no longer met my needs. I took an interest in pop music, learned to play chess and developed a liking for cognac, often concluding my day when my university grant allowed it in Le Riche café, hideout of the smart and fashion-conscious of Montpellier.

On quiet evenings Marie-Cécile and I would go to the practice rooms in the Conservatoire where I played her Chopin, Liszt and Beethoven. She in turn walked me through the streets of our adopted town and to every exhibition she deemed worthy of her consideration. Then when we had exhausted our surrounding area, we hitch-hiked to Arles, La Grande Motte, Nîmes, seeking lifts from Citroën trucks, Jaguars and whatever else would take us, to see Matisse, Miró, Chagall, Vasarely, Gauguin and many others. I still flinch at the memory of trying to remain upright at a table in the Avignon station café, one drink each to last the long night through. We had thumbed a lift from Montpellier to see the exhibition of Picasso's latest work from 1970 to 1972 but could neither afford the train journey home nor somewhere to sleep. We became for each other a powerhouse of ideas. We grew together in the unfamiliar.

For Marie-Cécile's part, I do not know if she ever inhabited classical music in the way I pursued an understanding of painting and the visual arts. But these were the foundations on which I began to build a self and emerge from a conflicted and bewildering past. I do know that in the course of her first year of dentistry she changed to Les Beaux Arts in Paris to study the visual arts, and has since become a successful artist, specialising in iconography, lecturing at the Sorbonne. We laughed a lot in that year. We were giddy. We tasted the dark side of alternative Paris. We grew to understand the realism of French cinema and the creative, subversive truths of French singer-songwriters. And I now take much pride and pleasure in my daughter Roberta's gift for writing and performing her own material in a different context from France, almost half a century later, continuing in the worthy tradition of Brassens, Moustaki, Brel, and the wonderful Sylvestre.

I arrived back in Edinburgh with deep reluctance and the earth irrevocably tilted on its axis. I gained a decent Honours degree. But my knowledge of French, the depth of my understanding of the language, its nuances, subtleties and dialects and my enduring love of them, and of the people of France, together with my wish to be one of them, remain. I gained from Marie-Cécile, from her family, from her confidence within that family, her trusting, reliable relationship with her mother and father, perhaps too from my life in France, a pivotal first valuing of who I was; of what I could offer another person, of what I could summon in that person to the point of changing the course of a life. I received that most precious gift from her, love and affirmation. In short, a life.

Les Tuileries, Paris

Your approach to that white painted chair
which had something of Giacometti about it
in a Paris garden without grass..
back end of arty...
is a precise green with white,
mild and magnificent
as well as your words and your hair bow;
and as you order your nougat glacé
gold rimmed and salon seasoned
you taste your every word,
and together with your grandson or so I imagined,
you gather the soft fruit of your vowels
lightly tread the idioms of your native tongue
speak with measured rythmns
aged in the casks of birthright and Gallic precision
and then the milk soft sun
moves on.

A Reluctant Homecoming

MY RETURN TO Edinburgh from France in September 1970 was bleak. I was dismayed at the shabby train in which I rolled into Waverley Station, the dirty ashtrays and spills on the tables of the restaurant car, irritated at the slovenly gait and unkemptness of the ticket collector.My overwhelming sense was one of greyness... the skies, the buildings and the people. I missed order, neatness and the precise presentation of those I had grown to regard as mine; slick serving staff who placed even the most humble coffee with flourish, as if it was a rare oyster to be treated with delicacy. I was disorientated by decimalisation, which had taken place during my year away, though at the same time glad to see the end of British quaintness. Most of all, I was sad. I had felt melancholy many times, but this was more an aching emptiness which had taken my skin, my stomach from me, leaving nothing safe or solid. What I had seen, touched, heard and tasted had gone, leaving only a hunger which I could neither feed nor share. The world I had created for myself in France disintegrated on arrival and the old, tired life I had forgotten for a time with all its darkness and demands, and which left no capacity for ripening was again present. It had not disappeared at all.

I was resolved not to allow my mother to own or reclaim me, and as she showed me around the changes she had made in our house, I countered her more within than without, armed against her softly seductive traps. Her worries and nightmares were hers and not mine, and they never were. In the days that followed I made the decision that to overcome my grief, I needed for the rest of my life to fill my days, to fill my wardrobe, to fill my home, my makeup boxes and my bookcases, leaving no space for thought, feeling and most of all, avoiding the slow movements of concertos and violins. I would take my life forward on one level, a daily dance of allegro, without much meaning... welcome the superficial... and the adagio of it, located in an underworld where I and my truth were to be found by me alone, furtively.

My joy and surprise at feeling that I had somehow come home in France had given me a perspective on my upbringing and my life in Scotland. All that France had been, now intrinsic to me, maybe it always had been, only hidden and inaccessible up until then, made me see things from a different angle. I had been in flight, for sure. In contrast to my own background, both Italian and Scottish, the dignified conduct of the French, economical in all things, especially in dress, conduct and words, delighted me. My regard and admiration for them was unqualified. There was so much I felt I could still learn from them and could be, with them. I wanted to go back, but there was the degree to finish, and there was my mother, and responsibility. Was she my responsibility? As she said, she had given up a great deal for me, 'made a lot of sacrifices'. Had she? And did I owe her for that? What does a child owe a parent? I certainly felt a grudging sense of duty. Added to that there was also the issue of courage to do the unthinkable. Was this a silly dream? To return to France, leave the degree, live as a musician and writer, commit to the smart, chic lifestyle. But I had little courage and I did not go.

The space that I gained did at least afford me the energy I needed to objectify, and so mitigate the oppression of my background and the damage it had caused. Through the anxiety of my early years and the constant confusion and questioning of my life as a teenager, I never could be, never felt able to be, skittishly carefree. But now very much aware and determined, I began to make my own careful way, defining me and my life amidst parameters, within the limits of duty and whatever was indeed my responsibility. An image of Michelangelo sculpture has remained with me through the years. His task as he saw it was to release the form that was contained within the block of marble. And mine was to emerge from the crushing needs and emotional requirements as my most authentic self.

I lived between realities, able to remove myself emotionally, find the cold spots within me from where I was often able to be directly critical of much of what I rediscovered, of what I had escaped. My homecoming and settling back was then an exercise in judgement and journey at the same time; of both pleasing and privacy. I challenged expectations of me, assumptions about me, since I was no longer the person I had been. I was resolute in deflecting the attempts made by my mother to deconstruct what she did not understand and to sabotage the determination she saw in me to desert her, my family, Edinburgh, and build a life elsewhere. I had no real fixed plan, no clear goal, only to find again that vision that I had seen on an afternoon after Matisse in Paris; to detach and to separate.

As the daughter from an Italian background I settled back into the home I was brought up in – there was no question of moving out – and into a mix of café life and university. I moved between these two worlds. I also began to see the man I eventually married, Paul Pia. My mother delighted at my 'normalising', at my relationship with a lawyer. This impressed her and at this stage in her life she welcomed the opportunities he and his family brought for her to socialise again within the Italian community... male partners to dance with to the music of the Paesano Band in the Roxburghe Hotel or Cinderella Rockerfella's; to make, along with a younger set of Italian men and girlfriends, a glamorous fun-loving group. She welcomed my social life into hers, the people and the parties that Paul brought... young professionals and respectable conservatives.

The dinner dances at the George Hotel, the balls at Edinburgh's New Club, the cocktail parties, drinks at the Traverse Theatre bar, also extended me, gave me a lightness, offered me a lifestyle I had never envisaged. With Paul the possibility of a life of my and our creation opened up. My mother also, I believe, saw this development as a means of rooting me in Edinburgh, which it of course did. The part that did not please her was my gradual distancing; the separation of my life from hers.

Things for me had been especially acute in the area of meeting and being attractive to boys. I was always the 'wallflower', the only one to leave a snogging roomful behind in a taxi home. The issue of dress and presentation has been a defining and complex one for me. It was only well after my teenage years that it became important. With hindsight, I see my previous nonconformity as an assertion of my personal freedom and distinctness from the rest of the family. While my friends and particularly my family worked hard at presenting at their best, makeup, clothes to flatter, and while I was conscious of the style and elegance of the Italians around me, I held stubbornly to being just me. The more pressure from my mother and her *maquillage* and from what seemed to me to be over-glamourised, over-presented cousins, the more tenacious as a teenager I became, and the more introspective and depressed I became.

Not very long after my return, there was to be a grand ball in Edinburgh's North British Hotel, organised by The Ice Cream Alliance. It was to be the social highlight of the wider Italian community UK-wide. Tony Coletta, my grandmother's nephew, was the retiring President. Paul was my boyfriend by then, for which my mother was thankful, and everyone else astonished. But I had come back with my hair completely shorn, a stylish look in France at the time. Every branch of the Rossi family, from Fife, Lytham, and Loanhead as well as a contingent from Huddersfield, had gathered days before. While the lipsticked female family members were planning a bejewelled, backcombed, lacquered and beautifully bouffant debut, my plan was cropped hair and round rimless glasses; my dress incongruously pink and flouncy. On the night of the big event, at my mother's bidding, and after some plotting, my eldest cousin Marie took charge of my makeup, grabbed me by the head, and stuck a small hairpiece on top of it which she then back-combed into position. And so, once again, obedient and unsure, I made my rather bizarre way to that ball.

It took until my twenties for me to learn about my own unique version of 'attractive' – never beautiful, though that is something I would love to have been. Once I discovered to my delight that I did indeed offer something sexually inviting, it became a truism. I worked on it, fashioned and developed it. I saw what pleased and did my best to match it. I revisited the family values I had rejected, and moved to heels, makeup and halter necks. My trajectory was from being an overweight youngster with flat feet and Gor-Ray pleats to understated French aplomb; to becoming in my twenties, a dramatic, lusty Italian woman, teaching the significance of the language of gesture and the Tarantella to my intrigued, amused but eager pupils. Though I still live the learned importance of presentation from my Italian background and from my French experience, I long every now and then, for those days in my two-person tent, my no-need-to-wash thermals, knitted hat, seeking out a shower and breakfast at four in the afternoon, content with sausages, oatcakes and a small dram.

The Copper Kettle Chronicles

IN THE YEARS we lived in Bruntsfield, my mother's world became increasingly The Copper Kettle café and the Italians who came to it. Even in the Morningside flat, when I was small, I had been aware of how much my mother's life was not in the home. She worked in the shop in return for our living in Grandma's house. We always had limited contact, my mother and I, and little or no intimacy. She did not hug easily. Then in the final stages of my grandmother's life, with Ernestina to help, my mother took over the running of our café, which meant that her entire day until late was spent at business. Sometimes while my grandmother was alive she and Ernestina returned to the house well after eleven, sometimes later. It was clear that together they had developed a lifestyle in that café which as the years passed provided them with some romance, friendship and social contact.

The café, which had been the focus of my family life since 1956, was both my home and a social space, a self-sustaining world, ever changing, ever nourished by the personalities of those who passed through and the regulars who inhabited it. It was known in the neighbourhood as the café run by 'those two Italian women'. Sisters? Cousins? No one knew. Many, I now know, had the disquieting feeling that somehow they, the customers, were not actually the main event and that there was something more compelling just out of the reach of their consciousness. It was iconic; a bustling, eccentric place of *italianismo*, of our dialect, our excesses; with crafted espressos taken standing up when we could encourage it, for we had created a social space with high stools at the front of the shop, Via Veneto style. It was too the scene of our conflicts: mine with my mother; and a place where my own were played out: the need for home and the familiar; a compulsion to reject that; to seek music, the arts and very different conversations; and yet to relax into easy repartee over the shop counter and a Fry's Cream bar of chocolate. There were the days when I would withdraw from life outside the shop, from challenge, and new ground, remaining safely shuttered within the familiarity of café rhythms and routines. There I would be inaccessible and protected and it was all easy. Then there were other occasions when I strode out, gloriously, confidently, ferreting, exploring, observing, finding new Edinburghs, new lifestyles, shunning the secure, in a new life adventure. I watched and considered them in the same way that I looked at a rail of new clothes; in the same way that I played with images of me through clothes.

The ethnic authenticity of our café attracted all comers. Family friends from the Italian community, the more liberal-minded, would drop in and idle away a few hours over a coffee. Because of my mother's marital status and her marriage outside the community, her relationship with her peers and other Italian families had been compromised and she was probably regarded as somewhat dangerous. As a twosome my mother and I, although the Rossi name was well established, were on the fringes of that network. Ordinary, respectable Italian women who minded their menfolk and worked alongside them in meek, plain overalls in the shop, viewed her, as a free woman. Her stubborn refusal to wear an apron or an overall confirmed certainly, my uncle's view of her as a libertine.

English was the language spoken by what was, in effect, this new race; but with that slightly mellow, lilting delivery of people brought up in a home of Italian speakers. I am in no doubt that there exists an Italian-Scottish way of speaking. As children they had grown up with one language at school and another at home. Like all children of non-English speaking families living in the UK they managed both, and often had the role of interpreter and translator for the parent generation. Such was its reputation among the Italian community that the shop even attracted a few Italian artists who were performing in the Edinburgh Festival and notably one season, the orchestra and cast of the Teatro San Carlo from Naples, playing in the theatre a few minutes down the road. They came for coffee every night which was exciting. Tito Gobbi, the famous tenor, and Maria Callas were also part of that cohort, but I imagine their preference was for somewhere much grander and altogether less couthy.

Edinburgh Scots, who were open to something a little out of the ordinary, came regularly too; and were delighted by it. For it was like no other Italian café they had ever known. Intrigued, they came back and back, found it increasingly irresistible and were soon drawn in from the periphery to the circle of friends; sometimes to our home where they might stay until the small hours; ultimately enjoying the exaggerations, the extravagance and colour of behaviour, language and appearance; the dramas, reconciliations; the tasting of homemade ricottas, the *baccalà*, marjoram and oregano sweetened white fish, the rich beef *sugo* made only with marbled hough darkening, softening hour by hour on the cooker in the back shop.

I remember being given a record player for my Christmas when I was a teenager; a clumsy, cumbersome machine with a powerful sound box. It was home to my vast collection of Sinatra LPs, EPs and singles. I still have every version of Sinatra songs, differently phrased, with different orchestrations,

Nelson Riddle, Billy May, Gordon Jenkins; on Columbia, Decca, Capitol (his golden years), and later on his own Reprise label. I was so well known in the record shops that they would routinely telephone me when a newly released album arrived in store. That machine was my maestro and guide, consolidating what I learned from others, from my piano lessons and what I had discovered in the concert halls: The Freemasons Hall, the Usher Hall, the Kings Theatre. At my mother's bidding, Grandma no longer alive to object, I would carry that blue and white record player across the Bruntsfield Links from the house to The Copper Kettle and when there were no customers or in the early evening only Italians, or when the shop was shutting, and the 'Italian boys' gathered, we would play the latest Italian hit songs, brought from Italy by one of them or ordered in especially by Jeffrey's record store in Bread Street. The streets of Salerno, Naples, Picinisco or Atina, left behind by the young tailors, hairdressers and cooks were conjured up in those hours in our shop. There were, too, the copies of the Italian magazines *Epoca* and *Oggi*, on permanent, special order from a newsagent in Princes Street, which my mother or Ernestina, leaning on the freezer, framed in a shop window of sweetie jars, pored over to absorb every scandalous or frivolous detail of the lives of 'stars' and Royalty. This was an ideal location at the counter for not keeping customers waiting... near the till and directly in front of the cigarettes, sweetie display and Golden Wonder crisps. There were stunning photo shots of Lollobrigida legs, Loren curves, of the mystical chiaroscuro of the Anna Magnani face and the assertions about Mastroianni and Bongusto, 'real men'.

The Copper Kettle era of magazines and the music of the San Remo Music Festival of the sixties was a time I associate with mixed feelings. Italian waiters circled in large numbers, finding their way to our café from the hotels and restaurants where they worked. As a result, my mother, from her mid-forties until well into her sixties (when she sold that business and opened a dress shop, her secret fancy) picked up her life, her autonomy and her confidence in The Copper Kettle. In that café, she recovered from a harmful marriage and took an obvious pleasure in being surrounded by handsome, admiring young men, the new wave of southern Italian arrivals. She was the envy, I imagine, of many and offended many more. What was not obvious to the world outside was the unusual dynamic of our café. What everyone in the Italian community including my own family saw, was a place where young Italian men gathered and where a much older woman was behaving in a way that was not decent, was unbecoming for her age and status as a mother. The reality was considerably more and also less.

Though late to the circus, I was a young woman increasingly conscious of my sexual power. Ernestina, for her part, was hopeful of a life partner and of soon leaving our home and becoming independent of us. And there was of course Alberto. I don't know exactly when my mother started her romance with him, half her age, twenty-one years old and fresh from Italy; and indeed it was at least that... a romance, for I later learned of them kissing, holding hands on Bruntsfield Links in front of the café, often when her help was urgently needed at the till. But I do know that it finally ended some seventeen or so years later when he left Edinburgh and his job as head waiter in a nearby hotel, returned to Villa Latina and came back a year later to a new job with a young wife. My mother was then nearing the age of sixty. She was distraught. Where before over dinner with him (he frequently took me out), I had felt sorry for his unhappy situation (my mother would not let him go he told me), I now felt both anger towards him for causing her such distress but also kind of triumph on his behalf and even on mine. I am still unclear whether that triumph was a kind of pleasure at retribution for the times when I had felt rejected, dispatched and manipulated by my mother and my grandmother (who was even angrier at this liaison than at my mother's marriage); that she was unavailable to me; or whether I felt some satisfaction in the rejection of this proud woman who was my mother, who was old, was competitive and who always assumed the sexual spotlight. She felt no unease at putting me in the wings, from where I usually conceded defeat. It was easier, has always been easier, when faced with the greater force of another will. At the same time, her tears at the loss of him meant that I was indignant and I defended her. I challenged him at Italian dances, if I met him in the street I confronted him. Her anguish disturbed me and her very public betrayal made me protective and tender at her helplessness. It was the final act of a life drama, of dreaming, of self-belief and romantic love.

When I reflect on it now, it seems clear that whatever the dynamic of their relationship was, my mother culled sexuality through stealth, forbade any of us in her presence, or indeed out of it, any hint of flirtatiousness towards the opposite sex or any kind of sexual innuendo. Much like the Queen of the Night in Mozart's *Die Zauberflöte,* who controlled all those around her, my mother possessed, dispossessed and disposed according to her whim. Her attitude to sexuality in others, a favouring of love as distinct from sexual attraction and behaviour, led to much confusion, guilt and repression in me to what later became strong, thrilling and compelling.

Her moods and impulses while she was in that relationship were affected by Alberto's behaviour. There were days when she was giddy and bountiful, suddenly shutting the shop when a few customers remained because he was hungry, declaring it family meal time and causing sudden rearranging of plans in order to appease. There were those after-hour visits when Alberto would come home with us from the shop, watch David Frost, Dave Allan, football or *Late Call* on television, and Ernestina was dispatched to make his sandwiches or even iron his shirts. Then there were the days when he didn't work, when he would arrive sometimes later than my mother expected, and as a final year Honours student, I along with Ernestina was under strict orders every Monday to chaperone; he, in his blue vw Beetle, she, silently raging; the atmosphere heavy and he saying absolutely nothing all the way to the lochs of the Trossachs and back. We sat behind them making thin conversation. These were uncomfortable and anxiety-provoking times for me. They were also frustrating times; disrespectful of us and especially of me, young, with a life of my own. At no time until Alberto left Edinburgh to marry would my mother admit the relationship to me, nor the very obvious and relentless disintegration of it, which all of us lived with and observed daily. Having witnessed the attraction and the falling in love at the very beginning, Ernestina had seen the good times while I only saw years of unexpressed rage and sullen, silent rebellion.

I was in daily contact in The Copper Kettle with some of the most attractive looking young men I had ever seen, and while I was a young woman with means, an only child from an established Italian home with the prospect of a business, in most Italian homes considered marriageable and normally sought after, because of the inherent habitus of our tight group there never was, strangely, any question of attraction. With the exception of my mother herself, and I do believe my mother's will was infectious, any romantic or sexual connection was unthinkable. Even more unthinkable was any possibility of an attraction between Alberto and me. Yet he liked me, I knew. There were only eleven years between us. I could easily have had an involvement with him. We often played squash together at my sports club, tennis in Morningside; went to the opera where together we saw the mezzo-soprano Janet Baker sing in *The Trojans,* Berlioz's drama about the Trojan War and we often went out for a Campari and orange before returning to the café for Sunday lunch with my mother and Ernestina.

Alberto's physique, his way of standing, tall and proud, his quizzical expressions, his shirt slightly open at the neck, pleased me. His masculine darkness, neat white teeth, his crisp, wry comments, interested me. He was handsome, especially in a suit, especially in blue cotton, and I liked being seen with him. He accompanied me one evening to an event at my school. I was in my final year, a time for boyfriends and 'dating', being seen to be attractive. As we walked to our seats, I was aware of my school colleagues and the nuns staring. I was proud to be with him. Happy to be observed. Best of all, I offered no explanation. On occasion I was sent to go and get him from work, (my mother's way of monitoring his movements, as I now realise), and he would take me to his room to wait while he changed out of his working clothes. It was entirely innocent, since those were the rules we had been given; and when I glanced over at him at the far end of that room, I allowed myself only a summary appraisal and only a little appreciation. I do not know what brief thoughts were his, but for my part I was the chaste young woman convincing myself best of all, neither admitting nor showing any interest in anything as weak, as unseemly, as undignified or as base as even a hint of sexual attraction. Bizarrely at that time *Gli Indifferenti,* the prescribed text I was reading at university by Alberto Moravia, was about the struggle between a mother and daughter over the mother's lover. If I did draw any parallels and if I did acknowledge and explore my feelings about Alberto to any extent, I am not unwilling but unable to remember. However I do know that there was no struggle and no tension; my mother could have her will and I would in time, in another place, rise to have mine.

Alberto was a beautiful man. He was good and straight-forward, polished and refined, light on his feet, intelligent and quick, his English was excellent, with a quirky sense of humour and an ability to pick up on the ridiculous. Most of all, he was tender. In my final year at school, I won a bursary from Edinburgh University to attend a summer school near Lake Garda. It would be my first time abroad and my first time travelling alone. I arrived too soon and had been in Garda for four days, alone, desperate and frightened. There was no one else living in the *pensione* I had been assigned as a prospective student. Such was my state of mind that one day in order to escape a stray wasp in my bedroom, I flew into the glass-panelled door causing the glass to shatter. My lifeline was the nightly tearful call to my mother from the local bar. Reverse-charge long distance calls were a complicated exercise then and I think the bar staff probably felt sorry at my distress and my deteriorating demeanour.

At that time, Alberto had been about to leave Edinburgh for Rome in order to make his yearly trip to see his family further south. Instead, he altered his plans, flew to Milan, picked up a car and came to Garda to find me. To my surprise, he appeared in the dining room of my hotel one morning. There he was strong, reassuring, smiling brightly. No fuss. Together we boarded a plane in Milan for Fiumicino, Rome and once settled, safe, I put my head on his bulky, warm shoulder and fell asleep. I remained with him and his family for six weeks in Ponte Melfa, the small village where they lived. It was there that I learned that lasagne is rather like a melting sandwich, the sauces of fragrant bolognese and bechamel only a light coating and a base for fillings of soft, pink parma ham, lightly cooked eggs or whatever else comes to hand. I also saw the glory of stale bread. When mixed into a salad, mainly consisting of overripe tomatoes, garlic, coarse salt and olive oil, that humblest of dishes tasted like nothing else I could remember. I recall too the warmth of a meeting, the strange look in his eyes many years later; well after the end of the relationship with my mother. He and I had been estranged for some years because of it. My family and I were at the check-out in a supermarket, when my youngest daughter asked why the man in the opposite aisle was staring at me. It was then that I met his wife for the first time and he my three children. I sought him out a few times after that where he worked as a waiter in the city centre.

What I will always remember most about Alberto was his protectiveness towards me, his appreciation of me expressed in a look and a teasing remark. Protectiveness was something I had never experienced and something I still often wish for. Above all his love of what was natural was so complete and instinctive. He was a man from the country with the behaviour of a gentleman. The last time I saw him before the stomach cancer, which I had known nothing of, was in his rented take-away café in the Powderhall area of Edinburgh. He was frying fish. This was not where he should be, not even what he had been. It was he who taught me that lemon juice is all that a steak needs, that to eat two cheeses at the same time enhances the flavour of both, that a cup of black coffee with a scoop of ice cream is delicious and that a peach is best eaten when left in a glass of wine. He loved what was simple and fresh... his sister's pasta, the air of his own mountains, the grace of a swim in clear water, the dry cleansing sand of the beaches of southern Italy.

On the Matter of Rooting

AS WITH PREVIOUS generations, the journey for young post-war Italians in the sixties and seventies to Scotland and into employment was made possible by relatives and friends arriving before them. They were the trailblazers and the foot soldiers; brave men, brothers and cousins, who came first to Scotland, or to Canada and the USA. My grandmother's three brothers settled respectively in the USA, Canada and Huddersfield, while her husband came to Scotland with Pietro Rossi, his brother. These first settlers, once lodgings and work were secured and opportunity became a reality... a business and a home... were followed within a year or two by the womenfolk and children. The considerable repertoire of Italian emigration songs tells many stories: *Terra Straniera* (foreign soil), a lament by immigrant Italians for the familiarity and beauty of home; *Mamma Mia Dammi Cento Lire*, the story of a young man asking for a few pence for his voyage to a new life in America, which I taught to my own pupils. Eduardo Paolozzi, who died in the nineties, was a grandson of Pietro Rossi, an artist and sculptor of international stature. Eduardo captured this pilgrim journey in his *The Manuscript of Montecassino*, an eloquent and enigmatic metaphor. The three-piece sculpture stands on the boundary between Edinburgh and Leith, where Italians first settled. They are a fine tribute to the endeavour, resilience and audacity of a new people, indeed Eduardo's and mine, who have over generations changed the country in which they lost and won, but nonetheless, in faith, invested everything.

Later immigrants to Scotland also sought opportunity, a living and a lifestyle inaccessible in the Apennine mountains of Lazio or the neighbourhoods of Naples. These young men, who spent many hours in The Copper Kettle, spoke with a great deal of appreciation of the freedoms of Scottish girls who could not resist Latin, fiery, sometimes tear-filled wooing and whose easy capitulation was unlike anything they had experienced back home. I was told once of a young man from Naples who, in order to prove his love for a friend of the family, took a knife from the restaurant table, cut his wrist and on the paper napkin wrote '*ti amo*' (I love you) in his blood. They would arrive on a day or night off, freshly shaven and glossy, tailored, mirror-focused, to have a quick coffee before a night in one of the city discos or coffee bars renowned for 'pick ups'... The New Yorker at the West End, The Pied Piper. For the ambitious though, some barely in their twenties, the overall goal remained to settle down. They invested their efforts and futures in Scotland and put Italy and all it had been behind them, whilst keeping hearth in their hearts. Sadly for subsequent waves of Italian immigrants, living in Scotland today, their future remains vested in the old country... where they build new villas for summer and old age and where in large cohorts, they return to from Largs, Motherwell, Tarbert and Oban every season; their sizeable cars and trappings creating an ill-adapted, overtly prosperous superculture within the modest Italian villages they and their forefathers left behind. It is not unusual for a BMW to be seen today, cruising the twisting roads, the streets of an Abruzzi village, or to be ostentatiously parked in the main square of Villa Latina alongside a ramshackle van full of farming equipment or a hen or two.

As a young woman in my twenties, observing the flow and eavesdropping on the confidences shared between my mother and Ernestina, I could see that for many, a convenient route to self-betterment was through a sensible marriage. Ideally, while their first years in Edinburgh were essentially a time of dare-devilry, many men ultimately found wives within the Italian community. If they were willing to toil hard, work with their wives in the already successful family business, good fortune and security through patronage were certain. This was an attractive proposition that would delight both sets of parents, the prospect of cultural harmony, shared values and similar attitudes to family assured. If fidelity was in any doubt, financial ties and legalities would guarantee the marriage. A sturdy son-in-law and a solid, dutiful daughter or daughter-in-law fully harnessed to their demands and that of the wider family meant that as old age approached, in-laws could step aside and have less involvement in the business. Either because there was on both sides an unspoken but acknowledged recognition of the difference between my own family, long established in Edinburgh, and the yet untried abilities of those new to the community; or because I had no aspirations to be a wife, or to work in a shop, this future was never in prospect for me. With much good humour, delighted at and appreciative of flattery, admiration even, I remained very firmly apart. For as is always natural to southerners, those from the *ciociaría,* the boys charmed with words and a wide smile, impressed with their stoicism, an ability to work hard, and their adaptability, flexibility and willingness to fit in. Most of all, they stood above all others with their energy for life and inquisitiveness, their desire to uncover, root about. In our café, the Cellinis, the Coppolas, Rizzos, La Grecas and all the Palumbo brothers, for example, noisy and restive, little boys grown tall, would pace the floor, tell a funny story, making light of problems with wonderful, good-humoured mimicry. Observant of the world, and especially as devoted students of human nature, Italians have that gift.

In my twenties, with a developing career and increasing distance from my background, having travelled, established new parameters for myself and my own anchors, I felt able to revisit my roots with safety and, to some extent, embrace them. Through this fresh influx of *italianismo* into The Copper Kettle and into my life, I was both pleased and better able to understand my native culture, my Grandmother and the Scottish Italians of my childhood. To hear and use the dialect in a context other than an intimate one resulted in my awareness of a language with character, distinct from Italian itself, and the strong personalities of the people who speak it. The language of Lazio and the Mezzogiorno, its words and syntax, the ancient proverbs from the folklore of the Abruzzi and Molise and of *viticusar*, my own dialect, are shaped by humour, and *furbezza*, cunning; by a philosophy which recognises and tolerates human eccentricity, natural impulses and behaviours. *Nella vecchiai, le cavze rosse*, red socks in old age disinhibited old age. *Chi me vuò cott e chi me vò crur*, some want me cooked and some want me raw, they all want a piece of me. *Iam 'n cul alla legg;* up the arse of the law, to hell with the law. *Nun ce mett ne sal e ne olio*, I won't put either salt or oil on the matter, or I'm not interfering, it's not my business. *Pe' conosce na persona ci ter a magna ne quintal re sal*, you need to eat a ton of salt with a person to know them, you never really know someone. *Vuò mette gle per n'coppe ogni pret*, he wants to put a foot on every stone, he will not leave things alone. *Chi se mett la camice pe la prima vod, se la cag*, he who puts a shirt on for the first time, soils it, it's important to know your place; and last of many, many more regional wisdoms, and one of my favourites, *e menud co' 'na man innanz e un adredd*, he came with one hand covering his genitals and another his bum. In other words, he came empty handed!

There were of course values that I observed even in my own family in how they conducted their personal and public lives, which I felt unable to share; that compulsive need to display wealth and success mainly to fellow Italians; that nakedly overt belief that it is money that brings social status; and a world view that through the material comes equality, parity, power and influence. If money is not enough to secure a firm footing in the Scottish establishment, then it will certainly buy the favours of an unsuspecting someone who is already rooted within it; the seduction mainly through hospitality of key figures, people thought to be important – the judges, the titled, the successful Edinburgh business community and always men.

There was, for example, the incident of the London trip when two uncles of mine decided to visit a noteworthy Italian, cosseted deep in his knighthood and London mansions, an establishment figure and owner of a chain of hotels. Rico had been interned as a prisoner of war with him some thirty years before for a short spell. The other uncle, his business faltering and once again close to bankruptcy and to Players No. 6 cigarettes rather than his cherished Cuban cigars smoked at the gaming tables of Blackpool and its environs, was seeking a favour. So he compromised Rico, begged him into renewing that historic and best-forgotten connection under the pretext of friendship. That open exploitation, possibly more a characteristic of Italians on the move, was in short repugnant to me, nothing short of demeaning. The Italian Scot, because of the necessity to survive, is maybe still in my experience, almost always propelled by economic interests in all things, even what is most intimate and personal. I see it furthermore as half a community, and an impoverished one where women's voices are absent even to this day. Their role circumscribed by prescription and convention, they are at best forceful within the home. Socially, their sole function is to wear a 'beautiful dress' and they are publicly visible only through men, a mere enhancement, and at best his echo. It was to this circle that I had returned and this circle that I increasingly sought to abandon.

But despite my indignation and too frequent outrage, as a young woman of the seventies and eighties era, I could not and cannot deny now my tenderness. Often I catch myself aching for a community that has survived, stayed strong, is delightfully and unapologetically human, so childlike and so readable. I feel so much warmth at the familiarity and predictability of it all... the weddings... the funerals... the chance meeting... and so much fierce pride and tearful triumph at the expansiveness, exuberance and at times overwhelming generosity of these, my people. At times, my emotions bent to the will of my thinking mind, I can stand aloof, fiercely critical of the kaleyard, the ghetto and the too familiar faces and unsophisticated voices of my childhood. At other times, I would and do return to the generous heart of a band of people I know by sound and feel, that I love; staunchly and reliably there. And I succumb secretly, guiltily, unwillingly, increasingly weakening at laughter, at a gesture I recognise, and every simple, honest word that brings me to my beginnings however stark. I was and am still made whole, re-affirmed, armed for the next stage. I have always been lonely, relentlessly self-doubting, only very occasionally fine with myself; a regularly anxious traveller. That has always been and continues to be, the dilemma.

Good Times With My Mother

I AM A lover of coffee shops. I seek out and keep them wherever I go. My phone cleverly homes into my city favourites like a dog nosing out its territory... in Edinburgh, Belfast, Glasgow and even the Western Isles. That sociability and daily banter of The Copper Kettle is maybe still an experience I seek. I have a daily need for a mellow, well-assembled latte among the cool, the creative or the intriguing. The experience often alters my perspective, offers insights, influences my clothes choice and even at times my identity, since I often like to fit in. My friends and those I invite to join me in my chosen haunts often regard my peculiarities around coffee as unnecessarily pretentious. But in my student years, occasionally while in charge of The Copper Kettle, or indeed doing paid work as a student in my uncle's café in Morningside Road, I did actually acquire the skills of a fine barista... the ability to create a froth, the spout of the steamer tilted at an angle to both move the milk and aerate it, and to carefully balance the quantities of coffee and milk with understanding and without much fuss.

I cannot say that I did not greatly enjoy my time in The Copper Kettle even as an outsider; some of it embarrassing, at times hysterical and raucous. These were times of tears of laughter, my mother doubled up and holding on for fear of falling over, the hilarity particularly uproarious at something silly said in the midst of a screaming argument. I was entertained and valuing of the energy and the flair of those that passed through. While I had not been a large part of the café life as a child, my mother took joyful account of me as an adult; of my freshness and new energy and they offered her something she had not anticipated. For my part, I got to know her, appreciate and enjoy her, though that route to our connection had been unusual. Through those that came, that loitered, and pottered, near the hot pie machine, the milk crates stacked at the door, and certainly through my mother herself, I recognised in myself a tendency, like the Italians I mixed with, to study people, to find the funny, to stare, to pick out the peculiar and the unusual in a look, a mannerism or a way of speaking or being... to *ripassà* or mimic. For Italians are inquisitive: *Chi si tu?* 'Who are you?', I was asked when I visited Viticuso after my mother's death and once they knew who I was, all was as it should be. They are, too, quick to ridicule, and merciless in their criticism. Ernestina displayed another typical trait in southern Italians, that of practicality and a resigned tolerance of human foibles. Always biddable, she would shrug her shoulders in that Italian way, *Che può fa'?* What can you do?, showing no surprise but simply mild amusement at, for example, my mother's unusual behaviour and often quite astonishing suggestions.

The house in Bruntsfield was a two-minute walk across the Links to the café. Always willing, Ernestina was persuaded by my mother to paint the floor of the bathroom in the house last thing at night before we all retired to bed. Her thinking was that the paint would have a chance to dry. Ernestina quickly expedited the job and went to her room to sleep. She and I were under strict instruction not to use the bathroom during the night, whatever happened. She heard my mother out quietly, as usual, raising no objection, for my mother could never be diverted from her plan. However, in the small hours that night, she did, perversely and unusually, wake up with an urgent need for the toilet.

She made several futile attempts to enter the bathroom and propel herself towards the toilet seat without disturbing us or her handiwork. Then, braving the hour, any potential assailants and the temperature outside, which was certainly cold (she was half-dressed), there was nothing for it but to use the public toilet just across from the house, which was a place for homosexuals in the area to meet, or to go the full way across the path to the shop. Avoiding further upset and further gymnastics with a full bladder, Ernestina resignedly put her dressing gown on, and doggedly made her way to the café. She was fortunate in that the neighbours were all sound asleep and there was no one in the police box opposite the shop, or any malingerer visible to witness her floating footsteps towards The Copper Kettle and the cold toilet in the back shop.

There was also the day of the explosion. Ernestina and my mother were both in the back shop and I was quietly reading. Ernestina was standing stirring a pot and my mother was seeing to her hair at the long mirror above the gas fire. Suddenly there was a blast and the oven door flew open. My mother charged headlong out of the door and into the street, clutching her poodle. Ernestina, her face glowing red, hair in frizzed threads around her face, tights hanging in rags round her ankles, was ever at her post, disorientated, stoutly stirring the pasta.

One of my mother's favourite customers was called Jack, who despite problems with his back and frequent visits to the chiropractor, had managed with Aileen, his pretty, precious but patient wife, to produce six children. He was the opposite of energetic, but I think my mother liked him because he was both sweetly appealing and always suggestive, which he was permitted to be and which made us laugh. We never took his offers of a kiss or a squeeze seriously, though I am in no doubt that they were meant. Several coffees with Jack would always relax and brighten the day. Somehow in his company everything would feel sound. He would shuffle in, wearing a shiny suit, probably recycled from years before, always oversized, and with his floppy, crooked smile, drink his coffee at the counter. But when things got busy, he would sensibly withdraw to a table. He had an eye for good looks. We spent several laughter-filled Hogmanays with Jack and Aileen in our home, the jokes ribald and the gossip at the expense of others often wicked. They sometimes came to Italian dances and Ice Cream Alliance dinners with us, though his style was always slow, a waltz and never a jive. I think in his heart really, watching him dance with his wife, he was a loving romantic who had only her in his affections. Along with others, including Paul, who was 'courting' me at the time, and various Italians, waiters, hairdressers, tailors, and shy new arrivals, Jack and Aileen made up the happy, raucous group.

Jack's business activities were somewhat dubious. He possessed a number of battered leather suitcases which he frequently took to Yorkshire, and I seem to remember a Gladstone bag. I also remembered more recently his admission that he frequently gate-crashed funerals for a free refreshment or two. Weddings must have proved a bit more difficult, since sociability and sharing details of how one knows the family are a requirement, rather than the recollection and discretion required on the occasion of a cremation or a burial. But it was nonetheless he, who gave my mother and me a taste for roaming in my second-hand first car, a white Citroën Dyane. On his recommendation we moonlighted often, to York, Harrogate or Richmond, sometimes even just for an overnight. There was no practice in the Italian community of exploring the countryside for the pragmatic Italian Scots, animals, nature, city and country, are seen mainly in terms of financial return or survival. But independently-minded as she was, and always the dreamer, my mother had a love of the quaint, the picturesque and the historic; the Shambles in York, the Minster and the Whip-Ma-Whop-Ma Gate where the city's whipping post and stocks were. A guide once told us that nagging wives were hung there, a spike under the chin, and should they utter a word, their tongue would be pierced through. These stories and this place especially would prompt a stream of imaginings and postulations from her. She was becomingly entranced. However, after several visits and armed with some basic knowledge of the origins of York city, my mother was suddenly and inexplicably no longer willing to stay in the dignified, costly Station Hotel which was close to the old city walls. She was, she explained, afraid that a gladiator would crash through her bedroom wall or that an entire Roman Legion would invade during the night.

There had been no encouragement in my mother's upbringing to read. Yet, unlike her brother and sister, more income-focused and more acquisitive, my mother loved books and I have no idea, I regret to say, where this interest came from. I can find no trace of it either in the Italians that frequented our home or shop. When I visit Italy, I do not see a society of bookworms. This is in contrast to France with its vast array of serious journals, trenchant cartoons, reviews and newspapers, its fine literary tradition which it has maintained to the present day, and where it is commonplace to see an elegantly suited man seated on a café terrace reading the poetry of Vinau, an award winning contemporary poet from Luberon or *Je Parle le Parisien,* a coffee table lexicon of contemporary usage of words with *tendance* (trendy). My mother encouraged me from an early age to read and enjoy books and as I grew, she sent me down various paths of surreal and highly evocative writing, Pearl Buck, H Rider Haggard, Daphne du Maurier. Easily terrorised she was very firm in her advice to avoid Dennis Wheatley! In particular, my mother loved the Brontës. So, during one of these escapades to the Dales in that little white car of mine, we visited Haworth. Only my poor mother, who was substantial, always following a diet, banana and milk, cheese and oranges, the horrors of the liquid Complan regime, and always high-heeled, had not only to exit the vehicle, but to push me and it up the hill of the town's Main Street.

I have no memory of setting off down the A68, which was the route Jack advised, at any normal time of day. It was normal for us to make our escape from the shop, leaving Ernestina in charge, towards the close of business at around ten, when things were slowing, checking into our luxury hotel in the early hours. That wild dash down the motorway, lights flashing in the dark, negotiating not two but three lanes which neither I nor my mother had ever done before, were exciting for us both. We both liked service and comfort and a suitable setting for our nail varnish and our coûture and so we chose our luxury hotels carefully. It was in York that we sought out the best gin and tonic bars, ate toasted tea cakes; in Wensleydale that we ate apple pie with a slice of local cheese on the top, not cream; and in Melton Mowbray that we sought out the famous pies. I think these were our best times together, getting to know one another, laughing mainly at anything that struck us as bizarre, and usually the behaviours of or what accidentally befell others. Our disagreements were like hurricanes, our subsequent laughter often exploding for no reason throughout the remainder of that day.

I will never forget one trip to Harrogate. Planned ahead for some time, this was to be a four-day event and having settled my mother's dog and done the necessary in relation to the running of the shop, we set off, unusually, in daylight. Just after the English border my mother unexpectedly ordered me to turn the car around and head for home. I tried to ignore this, hoping that her unreasonableness would pass, since she could give me no sensible cause for her malaise, but after several attempts from her to jump out of the car as we travelled at eighty miles an hour, I gave in and angrily turned back. I never discovered what had prompted this behaviour, but I did know her to be volatile and totally uninterested in what others made of her, childlike in her fear of the possible or even the impossible.

My mother was given to whims and sometimes enjoyed a cake or two with her cup of tea. She used to say that she did not like tea on its own. Despite pleas for reasonable conduct, from Ernestina and me, she was incapable of resisting an impulse. For instance, with the shop full of customers taking tea after the Sunday service or lunch, she would cheerfully advance upon each table, one by one, where a genteel clientèle sat astonished, as she prodded the cakes set out in trays before them, in order to find the freshest one to have with her hot drink.

Her best performance came one dark night in November 1976. By then I was teaching Italian and French in an Edinburgh Roman Catholic comprehensive school. My mother, now in her fifties, had sold the café, and was working as a temporary sales assistant selling bridal gowns. She hated both the work and the gowns, but seemed to have acquitted herself well, being offered the role of assistant manager after a few months. She had never had much time for marriage and far less for mothers with pushchairs coming into the café. Often, to their astonishment, she would declare it closed to bar their entry, or, having allowed them in, she would decide enough was enough and pointedly put the keys in the door. Ernestina had left our home to marry and was working in her spare hours at dressmaking and tailoring. We were adapting to life without the café, life at home, life without Ernestina to help with household chores and practicalities. We seemed to eat a lot of sausage casseroles cooked in a slow cooker until the grease marks on the wallpaper brought an invasion of mice. Most of all we both missed the wonderful variety of humankind coming and going in and out of the café. Movement, change and activity were all we had ever known. As an adult when I had nothing to do, or when as a youngster school had finished early and I needed distraction, the café was reliably there. My mother, restive, delightfully capricious, with a need for a public, glamour and the bright lights, found it even harder. The café had been her social life. Favourite customers sat at the 'staff table' in the wee nook behind the counter drinking coffee with us.

On that evening, in 1976, we had our fish suppers on the draining board of the kitchen sink – there were no working surfaces in our underdeveloped kitchen in Bruntsfield Terrace – and we were waiting for the kettle to boil. The doorbell rang. I heard my mother's hollow greeting. Then she entered the kitchen swearing. 'You see to the tea' she said quickly. She disappeared off, I assumed to entertain our guest, Tilde, a lamenting, tedious relation through marriage to Benny in Fife, my mother's cousin. Tilde lived in the future, full of plans about what she would do with all the money, the house and café that Benny, almost elderly, would leave when he died. In the meantime, while she awaited her luxurious, relaxed life without the demands of an ageing mate, she would turn up on our doorstep from time to time, in her thirties, no older, puffy-ankled, breathing hard, asking if she could lie down for a bit. I don't remember a single conversation between either my mother, my grandmother or Ernestina with poor Tilde. Benny, I imagine, with his inquisitive mind and an acquired refinement, must have, at least at some point in their lives, exchanged a few words with her.

The kettle boiled, I carried the tray of teacups into the sitting room to find our cheery Tilde patiently waiting, her feet up on a stool. No Mum. Where the hell was she? I went back to the kitchen, looked in her bedroom, back to the kitchen and saw one fish supper. The light dawning, surely not, she couldn't have! I looked out of the window. It was raining lightly by then and foggy. Then I saw her seated on the park bench in front of our house, contentedly eating her food, and nodding happy greetings to passers-by with their dogs; they, politely doffing hats, wishing her a 'Good evening, Mrs Rossi,' and all as if it was midday on a sunny afternoon; leaving me as the dutiful, unfed grown up!

My mother had never been mainstream and she was generally rebellious. She had had her own ideas from an early age. When gossip about her lifestyle reached her, she would laughingly bat it off with an 'Ach! Let them buy a programme!'. While she enjoyed the status of businesswoman and the sociability of café life, she valued catering and serving food and drink to the public very little. Like my grandmother who had the vision but not the education because of the times, the mores, the struggles of war, my mother was intent on providing me with the wherewithal and opportunity to move out of the Italian ghetto that still had her in its grasp. In her best years, she valued thought primarily, was known by those who knew and observed her for being liberal; she appreciated the painting Masters, adored Caravaggio, Canaletto, and was filled with admiration when years later, my husband and I took her to the Medici Chapels in Florence to see the Michelangelo sculptures. She herself was able to draw well. In her last years, she developed a strong interest in the history of Edinburgh.

Unlike my burdened cousins, backs bent to the manic will of parents trying to make a living, and the whims of the customer, my evenings, afternoons and weekends, my school holidays were mine. I had been given the gift of a passage out, upwards and most of all of distance. As a girl in an Italian home in the fifties, I was deliciously free from domestic considerations; never once kept at home to do the chores, as I suspect is still a practice, probably because my mother and even my grandmother from the country gave them scant importance, only an expectation that they be taken care of. As a woman with freedom, with a developing career, I reached up for a profession, groomed towards it by fine women who believed in aspiration and achievement; women who were as far as possible, in their time, independent of men to provide. In this, we all three, my grandmother, my mother and I in my generation, were both unusual and little short of outstanding in our purpose and resilience.

The A68

How well I remember this way and this road we chose
for our night escapes,
our journeys south
the promise of Scotch Corner
the smooth, easy tarmac of the M1
its warming lights adding glitz to your glamour
to your legs and your lipstick, to my fine cropped style,
my trophy from another life.
We abandoned our sleeping city,
leaving it to burrow for its dreams,
those prima donnas of café life...
the gruffness of Gaggia, toils of an ice cream freezer,
the fragility of espresso.

Maybe in those giddy days in the dales
and our search for a good gin and tonic
we were hoping for Hollywood, life in a Rat Pack
and one of us would be Shirley Maclaine.

Could we have seen me now, then?
My life's years piled high and heavy,
the flotsam and makeshift of my days
barely ten years behind the age
when you probably found answers
to the questions in our last conversation
you were so hungry to hear
you knew then how to recognise endings.
How easily the daughter becomes the mother.

Religion and Sexuality

RELIGION IN MY Italian home, as I imagine in most of the
others, was a question not so much of faith but of superstition
and observance. For my grandmother there were black
Madonnas, weeping ones, one in Lourdes, a different one
in Fatima, some were Mothers as in the Pietàs, others were
immaculate and untainted. One had been assumed into
Heaven, body and soul in her prime, another had died an old
woman. She went to Saturday night Confession regularly and
was stoic about Sunday morning Mass at eight. As a divorced
woman, my mother was not so well regarded by the parish.
Should she have remarried, she would have been considered
adulterous, and excommunicated. But in any case, the fact
of a civil divorce without remarriage still placed her in a
compromised position, limited her socially, and was unusual
for a Catholic at that time or indeed generally in Scotland in
the fifties and sixties. There was constant speculation around
her. But before taking the final step of ending her marriage,
she did actually consult the Catholic authorities who
sanctioned her action. Nevertheless, she took me to eleven
am Sunday Mass occasionally, however much depended on
the demands of the shop. I have a lovely memory, which I try
to recreate for my daughters at Christmas and Easter when
it is possible for us all to gather, of the aroma of *sugo* for
pasta in our Morningside flat, cooked by my grandmother
for lunch when we returned from Mass. This is a gift I want

them to have, a legacy from their Italian heritage. Grandma had all the insignia of her religion around her person and in her bedroom, where the statue of the Sacred Heart of Jesus wisely witnessed a great deal, I would say. Her rosary beads were never off her hands and throughout the day and night she continuously mumbled her *Hail Marys*, *Our Fathers* and *Glorias*. While I understand the mesmeric effect of incantation and repetition, the summoning of a more contemplative state, I have never at any time even in my most devout years, had any interest in the rosary. I could never wait to reach the part where the short end began and there were only a few more prayers to say. I have a memory of some additional finishing-off prayers and I liked these; the language of the *Memorare* for example. I also had an appreciation of the solemnity and poetry of the psalm, *De Profundis* recited for the dead.

We did go to Mass, but never as a family, because of the shop; and not regularly. At school on Monday mornings, I maintained a low profile at the inevitable questions about the Sunday sermon, which I am sure was noticed, and that reluctance to offer information probably did mark me along with other Italians. My cover had slipped though nothing was ever said. The nuns displayed the same monitoring of our state of grace when, as boarders, we went to weekday Mass in the early morning. There they sat, arrayed around and behind us, with an eye on who had and had not gone to Holy Communion. An absence from the communion rail meant something grave, a state of mortal sin, and the teaching was that if one died in that state, one would go directly to Hell, so the sacrament of Confession was imperative to save your soul. The key issue for pubescent, hormonal girls was, what was it that you had done that was so grave as to merit the status of mortal sin? Venial sins, minor aberrations, were not a bar to the sacrament. As we lined up outside the dining hall for breakfast after Mass, one of the nuns, a teaching nun as distinct from those who cleaned and cooked (ageing girls from Ireland generally), would conduct, sometimes in private if there was a need, an ad hoc interrogation-counselling session. The whole point here was, had you had sex and or were you pregnant? I have a sense too that Sister St Patrick, who dispensed our sanitary pads, closely monitored monthly demand. These were the main preoccupations of the goodly women in whose care we were, and indeed they were also our own. The 'how far should you go?' problem was always there. It featured in every conversation and teenage girl comic around at that time. There were random warnings about how far one should go and also about the irrevocability of getting something started; like getting on the big waltzer at a fun fair and not being able to get off when you felt like it. My constant sin was 'impure thoughts', and depending on the scale and duration of these wild wonderings and imaginings, I would sometimes feel unworthy and unfit to approach the Blessed Sacrament.

After the illness and death of my grandmother, my mother's position in the family had altered and, having taken over full responsibility for the café, her attendance at Mass was even more erratic. Sunday was the busiest day of the week and morning Mass was really out of the question, so devout until the freedoms of France, I would go alone every Sunday on my own religious journey. I used to like the choir at St Peter's Church and enjoyed the quiet time after Mass, when the air was still thick with incense. Sometimes my mother would slip along to Mass in the early evening. Sometimes not. She would on occasion feel the urge for Confession, but lost some heart when having gone to the Franciscans one evening, she declared that there was something she wanted to discuss with the priest, whereupon he banished her impatiently, saying he 'had no time for this', and gave her several decades of the rosary to say as a penance. My poor mother was both amused at his honesty and quite astonished. Her view of the eternal counsellor and healer, the benign priest was quite altered.

My moral education was an interesting mix of the nuns' ignorance, their lack of sexual experience, their girlishness, my grandmother's obsessions and my own inclinations. I had grown up almost exclusively among women, with my mother and grandmother, and later Ernestina. My grandmother had had I'm sure, a fairly rude upbringing in Viticuso. They shared sleeping spaces and they shared their living spaces with their animals. The village women bore the responsibility of assisting with childbirth, had seen the harshness and heartbreak as well as the relief of a safe delivery. They dealt with the old and the unwell, and the less appealing personal habits of their menfolk, brothers, fathers and husbands and indeed often the priest himself. They cleaned, prepared and laid out the village dead.

As a consequence both my mother and grandmother were totally relaxed about their bodies. They were neither covert nor prudish. Theirs was a different modesty, more a dignity in their bearing and proud carriage, rather than secrecy and covering up. There was a majesty about my grandmother as she clothed herself, and a self-respecting sensuality about my mother as she chose how to present herself. After all these years, I still remember the *viticusar,* dialect words for breasts, vagina and menstruation. They were well-used in my childhood home. We had no shower then and a bath was a once-weekly event, so my grandmother and my mother washed daily in the sink in our little bathroom, door ajar. I have warm memories of my grandmother getting into her laced corset... *na bust...* and pulling at the strings well into her seventies, then turning up her hair using a short wooden rod, finishing off with *4711 Eau de Cologne*; and memories of my mother heaving herself into her girdle, getting herself comfortable in her longline bra, while I sat in bed, unabashed, happily chattering to her.

However, in relation to sex neither were quite so relaxed. My grandmother's view of men, maybe not uncommon in her time, was that men were only motivated by their animalistic urges. She was equally scornful of wifely, domesticated women who were dominated by their men, calling them *'na pecora appress a n'om'*, sheep trailing behind their men. She was full of dire warnings about the evils of men, their dirty desires and cunning in getting what they needed. I believe she gave her poor husband and indeed her own son hard times, and was deeply suspicious of their behaviour. I never got the sense that she had been in love, although she enjoyed the admiration of men and my grandfather. As far as my mother was concerned, love, romance, and most importantly the fantasies of being desired and admired were everything. Sex was either unnecessary or too great a step after my father. I see the same peacock, the same haughtiness, wanting to be wanted but unattainable, traits in myself. There were only two men on the fringes of the household with whom I had had personal dealings, my father and my uncle, and I was afraid of and uncertain of both. I took these misgivings, reluctances and shynesses around men into my adult life, along with a deep anger at their power over women and the imposed roles that I had seen played out in my family. I was genuinely astonished to discover that love was not something that only women gave. I was surprised to find tender men and men who hurt.

Altogether, these were the incongruous starting points for my own sexual development and my religious journey. For they are very much connected. While my body and its sudden impulses puzzled me as a growing girl, throughout my life I have taken a great deal of pleasure in my female body. I like it and am on good terms with all of it, its products and smells. As Nagoski in her recent book *Come as You Are* states, 'all beautiful; all normal', even in the days when I have been more substantial than I am now. And because like the women before me, and unlike my Scottish friends, I take a very natural approach to my body, its needs and responses. I have had no problem whatsoever taking off my clothes in shared hotel rooms, in front of my daughters, in women's changing rooms or saunas; and abroad even in mixed naturist saunas. But my pleasure in sex, my aliveness to it and its possibilities, my blurring of the boundaries of sexuality, have been impossible to reconcile with Catholicism, and even less with my restrictive family background. Furthermore, theology and Christianity fail absolutely to offer me a suitable narrative for the unanswerable questions. Why are children born in suffering? Why is there no universal justice or reckoning for the evil that human beings do? If there is a God, why is He not listening?

The randomness of life is in total contradiction to the Divine Plan that Catholicism preaches. Yet I wanted and needed more than the material commodities from life. I was always deeply susceptible to what lies beyond the senses; whether it be in a church, or on a mountainside in Scotland; watching Machu Picchu emerging from the night clouds in the early morning in Peru; listening to the barely whispering violin of Menuhin playing the Adagio from the Brahms violin concerto. I felt a lump in my throat in the cathedral in Rio at the stained glass mosaics in stark, dark simplicity, and my astonished youngest daughter Sophie-Louise asked me if I was crying. I was delirious at the magnificence of the sun through the rainbows of light against white stone in the *Sagrada Familia* in Barcelona. And in Cusco in Peru, moved and yes, envious, at the powerful chorus of a congregation fervent in prayer, still believing, amidst meagre lives and unexplainable tragedy. Still, when I feel there is a connection between the truths of another person and me, my legs begin to tremble at the disclosures and the honesty between us. It feels as if the words have been dragged from my innards to the surface, and I am left fatigued and frail at both the struggle and the intimacy of such a new encounter.

In my twenties, after my return from France, I was in serious difficulties with Roman Catholicism and voiced my crisis of faith to my mother. This, she claimed capriciously, raised doubts in her own mind and she delightfully unreasonable as ever, blamed me then for her lack of religious observance. However, my last conversation with her two days before she died was about my certainty of the existence of a spirit within us that would live on. I remember the look in her eyes when I spoke the words. I have no idea why I raised it. She knew, though I failed to see, that her time was now very short. She died two days later. I was not with her when she died – after a fearful struggle, because she loved living, was strong, was very afraid of dying, and wanted me there. I was not.

The Loss of My Mother

IN 1992 I was working in Glasgow as a National Development Officer for the qualifications authority, having moved out of local school management and development to a key post with greater reach, and career potential. For this, I was greatly criticised by the wider family and friends of my mother who felt that because of my responsibility to my three children and my mother, I should be nearer home.

I was alerted late in the afternoon to a phone call from the hospital. My mother had been readmitted with kidney problems. When I arrived eventually, I had to wait in order to see her and when I was finally admitted to her bedside, she had a cardiac arrest. She was stabilised after some time and I was advised to go home and get some rest. That was the last time I saw her alive and I have to believe that she was aware of my presence. I left very reluctantly. My instinct was strongly to stay, to sit with her.

At around nine-thirty there was an urgent call to say that she had suffered another heart attack and it was felt best if they did not intervene. By the time I had freed myself from the explanations of the doctor and reached the side ward where she lay, I found a weeping male nurse. My mother had died seconds before. My guilt at my indecision, at my unwillingness to think the unthinkable, to take charge; at my going on the advice of the hospital so that I was at home when there was a call to come urgently; at my failure to push aside the people and the obstacles that held me back even at the last, obstacles to reaching that ward; the who and the when, their useless warnings, careless blindness to our urgency, my mother's and mine; my futile run through a last corridor; these remain rooted within me. Always.

There was a moment when my mother was staying with us, not long before her failing health became undeniable even to me, for I consistently remained blind to it, in spite of the evidence. There had been her sudden inability to walk far, her breathlessness, her loss of vitality all of which I brushed off. Had I stopped to consider it, I would have known that my badly concealed anger, which she must have felt and which expressed itself in irritability, was really my blind fury against the inevitable, relentless approach of her death; which she recognised, was afraid of and which in essence, she was appealing to me to stop or delay. But we did not have those conversations, we always dodged them in the same way that we avoided physical contact. So that when the signs of kidney failure appeared on her body, she hid them, above all, from me.

She was staying with us and sleeping in the bedroom that my youngest daughter later made her own, after her two sisters left for university. I came home late one night. The entire house was asleep and for some reason I went into my mother's room, which I normally never did. I stood watching her as she slept. I always liked my mother best when she appeared as she was naturally, unmade-up, her hair not backcombed but simply brushed, and I used to try and encourage her towards this without success. She was on her side, peaceful, pale-skinned (she had lovely skin) and childlike. There was always the child in my mother. I reached out and gently put my hand on her eyelids, for it was in the brown melt of her eyes where her vulnerability showed, her need for security and an understanding that she fiercely, warrior that she was, would not or could not articulate. She did not wake, never knew, and I went quietly to my room.

In Memoriam: Christine Rossi (1917 to 1993)
She Speaks:

my daughter, my daughter... All my eggs in one basket... all I
have is you

    let's go to The George
    you can't beat a good gin and tonic
    go and ask for more nuts
    ahh come on, let's have another one
    you're a long time dead

...I've only got you... all my eggs in one basket... given you
nothing but the best... a woman on her own... an education...

    can you take me to Jenner's Lancôme counter
    go and get the car
    spending money like a man with no arms
    go and stop a taxi
    no, no, no cream with hormones dear
    I'm a real woman
    no hair where it shouldn't be
    yes, a red lipstick... too blue... too orange...
    more pink...
    money doesn't grow on trees
    do you want us to end up in the poorhouse

...all my eggs in one basket... you are all I have...

    Let's get the kettle on
    I'm on a cottage cheese and oranges diet
    a banana and milk diet

will you come with me to Weight watchers
I like three courses, pasta, pasta, and pasta
yes dear, desserts... ahh, just get a soup plate
and let's have a bit of everything
is there a Kit Kat... a Digestive
I like something sweet with my tea
get some food into you
do you want to die of debility
will you please stop eating so much
they used to say I was like Rita Hayworth
when I was younger
all the soldiers fancied me
we had a great time in the war
dancing to jazz records in the back shop
I'm still a good looking woman
let's go for a drive
a wee *giretto*... see a bit of life
he thought you and I were sisters

...my daughter... my daughter... we're like friends... all my
eggs in one basket...

> shut the shop
> open the shop
> back in ten minutes
> closed on Mondays
> sorry dear, we're closing
> I'm seeing the bank manager tomorrow
> keep your fingers crossed
> there's just you and me...
> always keep the flag flying
> never let them see you're down
> hold your head up

that's the stuff
we're Italian... family comes first
it's family
the night Italy came into the war
they came up Leith Walk
a big mob
get out, Christine, get out
I was on my own
got out just in time
they smashed everything
nothing left
all the jazz records
I could hear them from up the stair...
Cab Calloway, Artie Shaw,
Stephane Grappelli, Bing Crosby...
though he was never much of a singer
it was his phrasing
they used to say I sang like Billie Holliday
she was divine

...you are all I have... I've been the breadwinner... it's not easy
on your own... bringing you up...

> go into the till and get some money
> run next door and get me some Otrivine
> my sinuses are bad... and Alberto vo5
> firm hold hair spray
> I feel dizzy...
> do you think I've got a brain tumour
> I haven't been to the toilet in three days
> get me some prunes while you're out
> no fish with bones... no meat...
> I'm frightened of choking

those mountains frighten me
I didn't sleep last night
I can't breathe... don't close that door
I'm not feeling well... don't go out tonight
it's New Year... a family time

...you are all I have, all I have... after all I've done for you...

engaged
what a shock
seven years
you said you would never get married
who will I go on holiday with now
he's just an immature boy

you made your bed
lie on it
what are you making tonight
call yourself a mother
you're a disgrace
you're not a real woman

...my daughter Anne... I'm proud of her... all my eggs in one
basket... all the sacrifice...

he was a handsome man, your father,
a wonderful tenor sax player
a gentleman in bed
I should never have left him
we wouldn't have divorced if I hadn't had you
he couldn't cope with the asthma...
Grandma...

I couldn't lead my life because of my mother

      I didn't want children
      all I've got... just me and you...
      me... get married again
      and rub some old man's back
      him coughing and spluttering
      I didn't want another man looking after my daughter
      after all the sacrifices I've made... a private school

fin che dura... fin che dura... for as long as it lasts we always said

        after all these years
        he was twenty-one... I was forty-two... a waiter
        we were the talk of the Italian community
        let them buy a programme I always said
        he's married
        bringing her back to Edinburgh
        I'm fifty-nine
        how could he do this to me

...you're all I have... all my eggs in one basket...

      look at that poor woman
      minding the toilets on Easter Saturday night
      stop the car and let me get her a box of chocolates
      it's the little people that matter
      always look after the little people in life

...you're all I've got... you won't let me die alone, will you...
promise me you'll be there...

The Oak Tree

WHEN I FIRST caught sight of Thay Nhat Hahn I cried. At first I did not see him but what made me lift my head was his presence. There was a shift in the air, or maybe it was the light, and I knew he had entered the room. I looked up; four hundred other people had turned towards the door, and the easy dignity in his movement and expression, his simplicity and grace, brought unexpected tears. I knew I was very close to an unquantifiable and unique spirituality which bubbled and flowed from within; which burned in his eyes; which found the void where I needed the most healing. And it was that softness, gentle on the most painful parts of me, rousing the parts which had numbed over time, that made me weep. Two slight-framed nuns walked behind him as he moved lightly up the side aisle of the great hall. He mounted the platform and sat for many minutes, while the room remained completely silent, all of us meditating with him and all of us waiting, hardly breathing; each of us strengthened by that common act and the shared emotion of being with the man, the teacher, the exile, the visionary and the 'gentle monk'.

We had gathered from each of the four centres that make up Plum Village in Middle Hamlet, near Bordeaux. A Zen Buddhist, who preaches harmony, mindfulness and peace, Thay Nhat Hahn founded his first centre of Interbeing in France, after his exile from Vietnam in 1966 as a result of his association with the USA, which he had visited several times on peace missions and on one occasion to meet Martin Luther King. He has brought to the West, and indeed to Buddhism itself, a clear message; a simple code for life, the Five Mindfulness Trainings; and with his community, a living testament to harmony between man and the environment, but more fundamentally, between people of different religions. His philosophy of Interbeing unites, within his centres, people of all faiths, Buddhists and non-Buddhists, Christians and Jews, all, who can and do freely, in conscience, commit to the sensible precepts for living set down by him.

After almost thirty spiritually fallow years, with an increasing craving in my bones and in my belly, as my life grew ever more secular and crowded, and as I cast around often desperately for something solid and enduring, indeed, an oak tree, I felt at last that I had found home. I had kept the fires at bay with my music, long-distance running (which had a meditative aspect), and fulfilling my need for my own company, often. But nothing engulfed me so completely as that week, walking with Thay and a vast company of others, sitting with him, praying with him and the collective force of us with him in stillness. I spent a week at Plum Village in November 2010. We shared rooms in stone huts with no heating. We ate sparsely and in silence. We rose at five am and walked in frost and mist to the meditation hall, with torches to find the path. We sat on cushions until our backs ached. We cleaned toilets, outhouses and kitchens. We were strangers to each other but we bonded together and looked after one another, because each of us had been touched by the unique, lifetime experience of being with Thay. I remember one morning towards the end of my time there, meditation done, sitting alone in the small sitting room looking out of the window as the sun rose over the fields, with a Bach Violin Concerto playing on my iPod. I felt the purest, most soaring joy I have ever experienced. I am happy,

I thought. I have that memory to sustain me and I bring one practice from that community. When war came to Vietnam in 1955, those in the monastery had to decide whether to remain a contemplative order or to play an active role within the surrounding community, doing whatever was needed by those nearby. They chose, rightly, to serve; and Buddhism which engages, acts and looks out instead of focusing on the 'I' and the technicalities of meditation, and indeed the elusive enlightenment state, is a central feature of all centres of Interbeing.

The great oak tree in Celtic lore has many associations. It is mighty, weighty, powerful. It represents endurance and Earth-based spirituality. It is above all, noble. The female equivalent, the Oak Mother, provides assuredness, safety, love and care. The oak has a cosmic wisdom valued by the Druids, who would only meet together if there was an oak present, and by witches who danced beneath its strong spreading branches, its leafy protective bower, and King Arthur's Round Table was made of a cross section of the trunk, so that he and his knights might be inspired in their discussions and guided by wisdom in their decisions.

In that week in November, I learned to put my forehead to the ground as a sign of re-engagement with the world before leaving my cushion, to touch Earth and reconnect with life outside the meditation hall. For we surely meditate in order to be truly with those around us. I did not return to Plum Village; there was no need. It had done its work, taken me far beyond what my culture and Catholicism had ever offered. I had travelled the years between my falling away from Catholicism in my thirties to the day in my fifties when I reconnected with my spiritual life, accompanied by the feeling that I was only living in one very narrow dimension; that half of me was dead. When certain triggers were present, I would melt with despair at the distance between what I was once, my expectations of myself, the years gone and who I had become. For there remained still that part of me which in my teenage years had glimpsed something else beyond the veil; a slumbering certainty to be nourished and substantially reawakened. But I gained certainty, assurance, and found my strength, my oak tree, there in Plum Village. I also found love and care after the childhood years and the loneliness. Most of all I felt safe.

Three years before going to Plum Village, on a sunny day in early June 2007, I found Holy Isle. It lies across from Lamlash Bay, Arran's coy, reserved neighbour. It is a land of wild animals. Eriskay ponies, goats and Soay sheep make up its indigenous population. It has been theirs for eight hundred years or more. Seals gather near the south side of it, cormorants come to dry their wings on its ancient rocks, eider ducks slip elegantly by close to the foreshore, oyster catchers make nests on the pebbly beaches and the odd basking shark has been known to circle its landing stage, where Jim ties up the rickety old boat called a ferry that brings you over at times to suit Jim and the tides. If you turn right after getting off the newly built pontoon, you will find yourself in front of the Centre for World Peace and Health, the main house; beyond it, still to the right, the squat, weathered boathouse, the island 'shop' and the scene of many a rollicking community party to bid a long term volunteer farewell; popcorn and kaffir leaves, poetry, music and song, for the island nourishes creativity; no alcohol, and only the natural exuberance, the energy and vibrancy that fill us all in such a special place. Above it is the Shrine Room, the spiritual heart of the island, where there is ritual and meditation, and beyond it a mile along the winding path by the glorious seascape, there are brightly coloured rock paintings to mark your way, a lighthouse and the retreat house for women on long-term retreat, of one or an amazing four years. As a former convent girl, I am well used to silent retreats since they are part of my past, and I am always interested to hear people and watch them as they discover this novel aspect of a spiritual life and become familiar with a new language. But I remain overawed, still cannot comprehend that someone might relinquish a life and the world outside for four whole years. This was a revelation. Go beyond the lighthouse and across the field up the hill and you will see a path to left, which will take you over Mullach Mor, the three hundred and fourteen metre hill, an easy walk for the fit, a challenging run for the even fitter. Some of the twenty or so long-term volunteers from many lands and a wide assortment of backgrounds, prefer to kayak instead; and there are even several hardy people, who have a daily swim in wetsuits on every day of the year. If you choose the other path you will come to another lighthouse from where you can see Ailsa Craig, and further along, Brodick itself. Beyond that is a sharp descent to a rocky beach where the ponies often like to idle.

On that first meeting, I saw a laughing Lama in sunshine yellow vestments coming over the meadow, a maze of gardens filled with vegetables and flowers buzzing with busy insects, a blue sea wherever I looked and a collection of herbal teas and home-baking in the house. We were taken upstairs by a woman who told us that she had a chronic illness and had decided to spend whatever time she had left on Holy Isle. The rooms were starkly pleasing, modern, bright and airy. This is a place, I thought, where joy and suffering share one space.

The following April I returned to Holy Isle to work in the garden as a volunteer. Something had drawn me back to the island. I had previously been a regular visitor to Samyé Ling, a Tibetan Buddhist centre in the Borders and the first in Scotland, dating back to the seventies. It was my first experience of Buddhism and where I first learned the value of meditation. The daily practice of meditation I found, calmed me and gave me great clarity as I neared the end of my doctoral thesis; it also countered my tendency to acute anxiety and panic. But this holy island had somehow called me. Here there was undefinable possibility. I liked the sense of leaving the world behind in a small boat, of being unreachable; nothing asked, nothing expected of me; all my roles fallen away – mother, lover, friend, professional. I was stripped and let loose. I disembarked there that second time amidst the flurry of unloading provisions, milk, cheese, butter and assorted bits of machinery and tools. All of a sudden as I stepped off the jetty onto the grass, there was the amazing sense that there was no other world, there was only here. Everything that I had known was no more. I had stepped away from tired normality and the drudgery of mainstream, the boring predictability of urban, to a fresh place, a different paradigm and another life entirely.

I would like to say that despite the back-breaking weeding in the kale patch and carting large stones in barrows to a grand pile in the centre for David, the head gardener, I gloried in the tasks. But it was a very cold spring that year and freezing rain descended on us frequently and sporadically. I could see it coming, drifting over the water towards us. I had not brought enough warm clothing. I was somewhat afraid of the austere David though I did manage to make him smile, probably at my lack of affinity with plants. I did not take to the work, but I did eventually relax about worms, beetles and other beings that scuttled over my gardening mitts. It seemed too that I had to gather an unnecessarily large quantity of kale to put on the table that night for community supper. But apparently that is the nature of kale.

However, in spite of it all, something powerful was taking place within me. Jose Saramago, the celebrated Portuguese writer, describes in *The Stone Raft*, a world where the Iberian Peninsula breaks away from the European landmass and floats off in the Atlantic Ocean. It is a schism of profound proportions, affecting every aspect of life, requiring a reordering of the institutions of a world society, of individual values; causing a new sense of home and solidarity between the Portuguese and the Spanish; and challenging the world community to rethink the roles and hierarchies of all of its nations.

The Buddhist world was very different from anything else in my history. The chapel of St Margaret's Convent, its candles, its soaring girls' voices, the jug of water for my morning wash and the narrow bed had all gone some forty-five years ago, and with it a religious intensity that I never regained. But here I was, after so long, returned to myself. I had travelled back to the spiritual place I thought I had lost completely. It felt as if I had not lived those intervening years. Saramago offers a very positive account of societal schism in his fascinating book; showing it as an opportunity to reinvigorate, evaluate, reconfigure, rebuild, and discover a new freedom. As an Italian Catholic, to explore Buddhism, experiment with it, inhabit it, enter its hallowed places tentatively, weave my way through its shallows soundlessly, for me, represented a cultural and philosophical schism. It was in the overthrowing, the uprooting, the extinguishing and the crushing of norms, language, understandings and ideas, where those who think they know you, have grown through the years with you, look for you as you stand before them and cannot find you, that a central part of me was reawakened. It was, more crucially, a means of reappraising Catholic practice and dogma through a new prism of thought and belief; all the while maintaining distance from both. Like a stone raft ebbing, receding, flowing back, homing, I have been able to visit and inhabit both versions of spirituality, attaching completely to neither one. But beginning, anticipation, fulfilment and completeness, a spiritual reconciling above all were there, present again in these sacred spaces, just as they had been in my early years before my life had started. They were in the early morning just after sunrise when the island is soft and still before it wakes; they were in the mists of dew when they fall light on the grass and sparkle in a new sun; or at dusk, when the birds and insects are finally silent, the gardens closed down, the sky a theatre of colour and the island offers its gifts to you alone. Instead of a chapel crucifix, an altar, there was a garden by the sea. Instead of statues and incense, stations of the cross, there was only the earth, the trees and the hill high above me. I felt the island quietly, calmly, bringing the migrant, somewhat sad with guilt, loss and disappointment into itself.

Not long after I left Plum Village, I became a Buddhist and found a route to a broader, more encompassing spirituality; not through the old, narrow Catholic way of my childhood, the unquestioning faith of Irish nuns, the mix of fear, superstition and pragmatism that was Italian Catholicism (pay the priest well, feed him and you will get a good sermon... a fine funeral); not in the detail of Buddhism either, the chanting, the one thousand daily prostrations, the effigies and rituals of the Tibetan tradition, its hierarchy and its patriarchal paradigm. But very similar to my relationship with both my Scottish and my Italian heritage, where I cannot or will not commit fully to either, but hold to both, the new understandings, revelations and insights have come from my constant migration from one to the other.

My Taking Refuge ceremony took place in the Shrine Room on Holy Isle in 2012. When I travelled over, having come from Kildonan that summer, the June weather was beautiful. The Shrine Room was festooned with flowers. I had chosen my outfit carefully, and was feeling a little nervous but mostly happy. I spoke my vows in Tibetan. I had talked at length and in depth with a vibrant, imposing Lama, with whom I related easily. She had a worldliness and a pragmatism that I valued, and someone told me that she had been a political activist in the streets of Paris in 1968 during the student protests. Most of all, humour aside, forthright and intuitive, she had a lively, incisive mind and a towering intelligence. She had the ability always to unsettle me. Which made me laugh with surprise and which I valued, for I wasn't accustomed to that kind of personal challenge from someone with whom I was not intimate. I had some reservations about the dogma, which I was and remain open about, but my reading over years, my Plum Village experience and the wonderful feeling of wholesomeness and healing that I had whenever I visited the island, made the commitment feel undeniably right.

I have gone to Holy Isle these past years to work in the kitchen, not the garden, for spells of one or two weeks, twice or even three times a year. There have been many remarkable and amusing events in that time. One that immediately comes to mind is the charming old lady who came for the winter retreat, but became so stuck on feeding all the birds of the air that she would come to the kitchen each morning to request bread, when she should have been at some devotion or other. Sweetly obstinate, it proved impossible to persuade her that the birds were used to finding their own food and were to be left to do so. Feeding them was not in their interests. She was dilatory in involving herself in the religious practice she had signed up for, to the frustration of her mentors, and was reluctant to go home for fear that the birds would starve without her. That same winter, a seagull who had taken to sitting on the wall outside the house, attacked an unsuspecting guest who had come out for a breath of air, after a teaching in the Peace Hall. Normally gulls are well enough behaved, except of course if they decide to lay their eggs in a nest near the walking path, and you happen along it. Unknown to him, another guest on the course had decided to give the bird a daily treat of sugar. The clearly addiction-crazed seagull, expecting his usual dose and not getting it, visited his frustration on the poor innocent retreatant. Most recently, there was the foal abandoned by its mother. While she peacefully grazed further down the field, her new-born was so weak with hunger it could not stand. It needed the milk she could not produce. There followed a great flurry of goat's milk purchased over in Lamlash, milk bottles and duvets from the house to keep him warm in the field and, should he not last the night, to help him die in some comfort. By the following morning, he was still barely alive. The vet, who had been put on alert the previous night, was summoned to come and take him off the island. But he had sourced another foal, with whom the young Holy Isle inhabitant could grow up and happily integrate into a new community of horses.

Everything that nature offers in all weathers, even in darkest January, is a joy on Holy Isle. But I have found equal happiness through those individuals whom I have met and worked with, some of them long-term residents. There have been low points in my life when I have considered that option myself. For whoever is there, whatever the changes, a new polytunnel, a new meditation platform or a curry plant as a garden addition, it is home. I have visited Holy Isle often after major life events, difficult times, often feeling insecure, bereft and disorientated; sometimes grieving and often just worn out. At those times, I have slipped on an apron, thrown myself into preparing vegetables and washing dishes, taken long walks to the faraway lighthouse, or on the day some years ago when a good friend died, up the hill with a complete stranger. I have always found reassurance and healing from this community of people from whom I learned to knit socks, with whom I have shared a much prized bar of chocolate or sat eating lunch in warm sunshine at the side door of the dining room, having just finished a shift. Nothing needed to be explained or said. I have found brave, wonderful laughter, lightness and depth in people who have survived astonishing histories, or who are still grappling with a past that will not let them go. There have been life stories which have brought me to tears, humbled me and profoundly shocked me. And then again, there have been the warmest most genuine hugs followed by, on one occasion, a merry dance around the kitchen and a potato cake. We are all of us survivors. I have come to realise that to struggle is something we all share, and that struggle and survival are what connects us as human beings. I have appreciated the enormous tolerance of people's moody, unsocial and unpredictable behaviour when they are in the midst of that struggle. Their colleagues work around it. There have been times when I have been irritated by a habit or a way of dealing with things, and when told why, I have felt unworthy, realising that I have some way to go to be truly compassionate.

Compassion, a Buddhist way of being, was not something I ever experienced in my own family background, which tended more to a mixture of sometimes cruel amusement and sharp criticism, which has made me self-conscious all my life. I also have never met an Italian who is part of a club or commits to regular attendance at any event. If there is a scout movement in Bari, Sicily or Naples, I would be very surprised. Discipline and regularity are not, I believe, traits of Italians even in the North, where the French and the Saxons have left their mark. My life therefore as an Italian Scot has been a combination of reliable regularity, a cultural imposition through mixing with Scottish friends and my professional life, as well as complete unreliability - my natural state. I have had many projects – boxercise, lute lessons, bagpipe lessons (though I never got as far as putting my hands on a set), drawing classes, golf and squash lessons; and writing groups of all sorts. I have been a paid-up member of the Conservatives, the Liberals, Scottish Labour and currently SNP. I have started Gaelic lessons, Arabic, Spanish, German and did actually manage to sustain a year of Russian. I approach things as an educated Scot and often behave like an Italian. If it rains, I won't go. If my daughter wants company, I won't go. If I want a good dinner and a glass of wine, I won't go. And if I decide to have a day in York, my evening commitment will not deter me. My approach is individualistic but my enthusiasm is genuine and I can be staunch. There have been certain things which have stayed with me. Playing the mandolin after a long break from making music is now once more part of my life. Distance running, which I did for over twenty years, was a wonderful source of fulfilment. And Buddhism, now central to my belief and way of life for ten years accords absolutely with my experience; this discovery; a Celtic Llama's flush: the oak's new leaves mid-season and a new start. But my beliefs are a random mix. I do not accept reincarnation; my practice is erratic; while I meditate, it is never a regular pattern, and I will not join in many of the ceremonials on Holy Isle or elsewhere, because they distress me and make me feel uneasy. If anyone asks me what Sangha I am part of (a local Buddhist group which meets weekly to talk, support and meditate), I choose not to have one. My Sangha, if anything, is Holy Isle and that small community. When on retreat two years ago, I caused much consternation among my supervisors one morning after breakfast in the dining room, when all the others had gone to their rooms to meditate, by boldly listening to Beethoven Piano Concertos with headphones on. To my mind Beethoven is a spiritual matter. They were unconvinced. Worse still, without asking, because it was the day that it was and Jim's tiny craft was at the jetty, true to my kinsfolk, I took a day off to go and eat mussels and have a grand glass of wine across the water.

The *Mammissima*

I CANNOT COMPLETE this account without some reference to my beloved Dante Alighieri: the most evocative imagery of the *Paradiso,* all light and sound; the most humorously wicked insights into human foibles and weakness in the *Inferno* and *Purgatorio*; the tender, heartfelt descriptions of the pain and suffering that come with regret at the wrongs that we do. All of human nature is contained there, so much so that in one circle of Hell we actually hear Dante himself collapsing: '*Caddi come corpo morto cade*'. The lilting triplets of the *terza rima* waltzing you from stanza to stanza to the definitive pause of the last line of the canto before you move on to the next adventure; and the most lyrical invocations of rousing, intoxicating joy that transcends the corporeal, dissolves all that is concrete, and takes you journeying with the great master, far beyond your frontiers of imagining and hope into a new place of vision, light and sweet, giddy music. All of this is to be found in Dante's amazing *Divina Commedia*. His masterpiece, that loses little in a decent translation, tells his story of finding his way out of a disturbing scenario, a *selva oscura*, a dark wood, and his ascent to understanding, acceptance and peace. There are many, many turning points for him, many defining experiences, many sudden realisations on his travels upwards to sublime reason and brilliant radiance, to his arrival home, and to finding truth and fulfilment through the loving guidance of gentle Beatrice.

This very tentative work of mine, written for Camilla, Roberta and Sophie-Louise, my daughters, also describes a journey, my own one, carved from a similar place of confusion. More especially, it is my journey of distancing from self-dislike, from the feeling of being unlovable, to a feeling that I matter; that I am beautiful and good, that people are grateful that I am around, that I add something to their lives. For in my early years, I had none of it; and through the years, from earliest times, from the impossibility to the certainty, that out of everyone in the room, he or she, she or he, would maybe choose and fall in love firstly and only with me. Stumbling forward, digging, foraging, colliding and raking through my mind and feelings, I designed that journey. I tried to find a positive narrative for every experience. I learned from them all and mostly from the bad ones. From the few shreds of confidence within me, believing in whatever encouragement I got, words, an expression or the look in the eye of a teacher, a friend, a kindly adult from that other community and not that of my birth, I found the strength to move away and beyond what was toxic and negative; moving upwards, building on those faint traces, making a life, and an increasingly solid self.

The writing of this book in itself has been self-making, a hard process of reconciliation mainly with myself, and also with the world, the one I was born into and the one I have lived in. The writing has brought perceptions and insights into my choices and what I rejected, seeing my journey as affirmation, putting things in order and in their place. I have been weakened, and at times strengthened, heartened and amused. There have been few of my questions left unanswered, however painful the realisations. In talking about it to close friends and family, I have been tearful with laughter; at other times, at my desk or in some coffee shop, I have stopped writing, sat back, trembled at the enormity, at the unexpected admissions, unable to stand up. Whatever else that can be said about this discourse, it is at least honest.

I have described this building of a self in each of the scenarios charted in the individual chapters... the enormous influence of my Italian grandmother, a wise wartime survivor, for she offered both a structure and a vision; the effect on me of the males of my childhood, crude, violent, disrespectful of women, and only by virtue of their feeble gender, their attempts at the subjugation of us women who were more able than them. I have talked about my conflicted relationship with Italy, my adoption of Scotland and my choices as to how to fit with that other society; my clear view of the imperfect norms of both and the limitations of each respective culture; my undeniable ethnicity, my rejection of it, my decisions as to what I retain of it and what of it I proudly present to the world, my unconscious acting out of it; the power of my French experience, how it changed my life through a first valuing and love of me and the learning about so much of life that came with it; my contested relationship with my mother and with those around her, our love, together with our resentments; her and my failures each of us to the other, mother and daughter both; my spiritual awakening through boarding school, music, song, by way of a discipline that through containment, like slow Mozart, leads to a beautiful blossoming of emotion, of soul and eruptions of sensuality; my convent education, the people within it that showed me another way of living, a refinement, a civility; who gave me poetry, music and art; and my path from there to Buddhism, to a clearer eye with which to see.

And now, finally, I turn to the task of describing my womanhood, complex, profoundly personal, exposing, but it is what I must do for this account to be authentic and truthful, and of the ultimate defining experience of motherhood. In the first canto of *The Paradiso*, Dante is overcome with awe at the task facing him, of trying to quantify the most absolute, intense loving experience of his life journey. Before he begins the climactic, final act of his poem, he invokes the help of Apollo, son of Zeus. I am not sure how much Apollo actually helped out as bidden, for I believe that the masterpiece that Dante left us is a testament to his own genius and not that of a Roman god, despite his association with all that we find in *The Paradiso,* music, poetry, truth, prophecy and healing. But as for myself, I certainly know how inadequate I feel at this moment.

On a recent holiday to Nice, I remembered a game Ernestina used to try to teach me and which I had seen her play with some of the Italian waiters who came to our café in Bruntsfield. It was called *par e spar,* odds and evens; a game played by two people by throwing up one, two or more fingers of one hand. What made me think of it was something I read about *Niçois* customs: the *mourra dei quatre cantouns,* which must have been the origins or a derivation of Ernestina's *viticusar* game. Only this *nizzarda* or *niçois* game, a relic of when Nice was part of Savoia, an Italian state before 1860 and the subsequent unification of Italy, required some skilful strategies including a constant shouting out in dialect in order to upset and distract your opponent.

Cultural legacy, practices and traditions become modified as they pass from generation to generation and from country to country, as national frontiers alter and as people migrate to new places and adapt to foreign environments. But there remains a recognisable trace of the essence of the original ritual, institution or ceremonial. So it was with Ernestina's game from Viticuso, a version from the hills of southern Italy, another perhaps in the north, though I have some difficulty imagining such unruly behaviour in the palazzos of Venice; and a more sophisticated form in Nice, now in France, and spoken in a dialect which is neither French, nor Italian nor even from Frosinone, but with a little effort, understandable in all three. *Mammismo,* the mother phenomenon, is one such pillar of Italian life.

In my family living in Scotland and in other such families, womanliness – I am deliberately avoiding the term femininity, which for me has distasteful connotations of pink, lace, muff and fan – itself bore a different complexion from certainly Scottish urbane norms and the Italian wives whose natural habitat and domain was the kitchen. If Italian women did go to business, rather than making the *sugo*, it was to 'help in the shop', to support men, take the strain off their children. The women who peopled my life as I myself grew to be a woman were very different, above all, strong, capable and people on whom others relied; not in a solid, quiet, constant way, not as the unheralded heartbeat of the family, the arms that warmed you when the world was cruel; not as weak dependants on their protective, male provider but as, if not the main breadwinner, at least an equal contestant in the tough arena of survival in business in a foreign country. For as I remember it, Scotland remained alien to Italians for some twenty or thirty years after the war and Italians to the Scots, and it maybe still is so. As far as the intimacies of family living are concerned, cultural differences remain: Italian attitudes to the young, fierce and passionate; and the old, honoured and cared for within families; sexual stereotyping, the tough demands of *figura* in all things; the importance and place of friendships within family structures, for male business associates apart, they are always secondary to family concerns and are played out at a distance; and what and how much is placed on the table for family and friends. I am still astonished at the notion that five hundred grams of dry pasta might actually feed four people, and that a welcome home in a Scottish household might be a cup of tea and not the biblical fatted calf. These women, my women and not the men, were the protectors, the ones with acumen and enterprise, the beacons to which everyone was drawn, the intrepid. Rather than coddle, they spoke proud obstinacy, resilience, retaliation and cunning vengeance. They were and are physically robust, energetic, intoxicating, charismatic, with an unschooled earthy laugh, not curbed to suit the genteel. They neither giggled or tittered, were neither attendant on the attention of a man or hopeful of being plucked, for if they wanted him, he would be theirs. Business dealings apart, when they were delightful and where necessary coquettish, for that wore well with Scots masculinity, they certainly made no attempt to please. Like my mother, my grandmother too had young suitors after the death of my grandfather, men who attended her but who never got close.

Like all the women with whom I have been close or friendly in my own life, all those I grew up with, mother, grandmother, Ernestina and my Auntie Louise whom I respected and valued, had deep voices that emanated from the belly; it was their hips they swung as they danced, or moved, their cadence in tune and rhythm with what lies below the waist, rather than limp arms-in-the-air motions which distract from what it is all about, rather than draw you in to what it is all about. I remember Grandma's beguiling walk across the floor of our sitting room when I was twelve, three books on her head replacing the pitchers of water she once carried in another life. I still see the tilt of her bosom, the slight turning away of her head, the arch of her brow, as at the age of seventy-five, she demonstrated the *ballarella,* hanky in hand, for touching was not permitted. It was an old dance from the festivities in Viticuso on the feast day of the patron saint, St Antonino. Likewise, my mother's tango was effortlessly alluring. She was not led but in equal control, her teasing power in synchronicity, in the tantalising mere suggestion of an embrace. And at the end of their lives, both women still had a full, responsive engine in their butts. In Cordoba, some years ago, I went to see authentic flamenco in a cellar. What still stands out for me is the sheer sexuality and animal beauty of a woman dancer in her sixties, haughty, commanding, voluptuous, barely moving, young men at her feet; her wildness was seasoned, sophisticated, quivering in the curve of a foot and the devastating charge of a beckoning fingertip.

I have never aspired to be feminine, but only to feel comfortable as the woman I am, to be tolerated if not welcomed, raw, unfiltered, unfussy and like the women before me uncompromising in my audaciousness. In every case, each of these women in their generation, took the family forward and a step further in from the margins. I like to think that I and my girls completed the job. My mother, in the end, deserted a life of the daily deliveries of two dozen rolls and a dozen Scotch pies from Irvine the baker, the moody milkman who always confused the quantities of silver, red and green bottle tops and the café letterbox, which was conveniently located for passers-by to relieve themselves as they wended their drunken way home after a night out. She broke free and ran a women's clothing shop for the better-off. My grandmother was the driving force who took the family from Bonnington Road up to Leith Walk in the war years, and eventually out of the ghetto where immigrant families arriving in Edinburgh first settle, on to bourgeois Bruntsfield and the south side of the city. Ernestina reinvented herself, becoming a dressmaker and owner of several valuable residential properties, and ran a thriving business. My Auntie Louise moved the family from ice cream stalls on Blackpool beach, amidst donkey rides, seamy sideshows and fortune tellers, to owning a large restaurant on Lytham Green, which was frequented by notable show business people, including famously, Frankie Vaughan, who became a good friend; and then she moved on to managing and catering in the many outlets of the largest park on the Fylde coast.

My legacy from them was in fact a great problem to me when I was taking my first steps into relationships and socialising, for these women, highly respected as business women, were unusual in the Italian-Scottish community and indeed in Scotland and Northern England too. With young Scottish people, I felt I had either to hold back (because who I was was unattractive), or else adopt the trappings of feminine flirtation and behaviour that I saw in other girls around me, which seemed to work but sat grossly on me. Nor did I fit Italian circles because of my 'peculiar' interests, neither business nor the home. I repudiated wifeliness as a set role and an achievement; and I rejected, in equal measure, church organs, a leap up an aisle, white dresses, a diamond engagement ring and a pram with a pink or a blue baby gracing my otherwise empty life. I saw these goals that other girls in both the Scottish and Italian communities aspired to not as lifetime objectives, the crowning of womanhood, but as part of the flow of a life, irrespective of gender, in which career ambitions, intellectual fulfilment and artistic expression play an equal part. There was no reason why all of these things could not, cannot co-exist in a favourable setting and which I could not inhabit as the woman I am, rather than fashioned by the norms of an Italian community or what I saw as the equally stereotypical, over-contained Scots I met and mixed with.

It might have helped my understanding of how to be with men, had I been more open about my interest in sex, but my family culture and my repressive convent experience with its bizarre versions of the mechanics and social conventions of sex, played their part in silencing me and modifying my actions. So in relating to men as either an equal, or as better equipped intellectually, and often socially too, I found I was impatient of blundering boyish inexperience, and I did not do well. It was only as I grew in confidence after my time in France and subsequently professionally, that my dealings with them improved, indeed were successful, for I had learned some of that peculiar language of foreplay and suggestion and I had begun to believe in myself as attractive. Female capability, women who made a difference, women who challenged expectations, were undaunted, indomitable, inventive, in short, fierce womanliness, were the woman I learned to be and my starting points for mothering.

In his recent book, *The Italians*, John Hooper refers to the ageless and still common phenomenon of *mammismo*, the cult of the mother and son, which he describes as a 'pandemic'. Indeed it is claimed that thirty per cent of marital breakdown in Italy is due to the role and power of mothers over their sons. It is impossible not to notice the sweet, passionate outpourings of love and yearning of a man for his mother in Italian song. As for fathers, there is only one song I know of , one which my mother loved and was her only ever reference to the huge loss of her own father, during the war: '*O Mio Babbino Caro*', 'O My Beloved Father', from Puccini's *Gianni Schicchi*.

D'Agostino (2008) sees the problem of *la mamma* as men putting their mothers first both in their affections and in their priorities. Jake Wallis Simons in the *Telegraph* in 2014, defined the issue as 'the Italian bond of love between a man and his mother that chokes romance, inhibits sex drive and even has the power to slow the economy'. There is certainly a kind of religiosity about the love of an Italian man for his mother; a sacred and childlike devotion towards a kind of Virgin Mary in human form, requiring his reverent obedience and protection. I was in Bari one summer holiday in the eighties with my husband and daughters. We decided to get tickets for *Cavalleria Rusticana* and *Pagliacci*, a double bill of opera. The most poignant moment of the entire evening was the final farewell between a mother and son as he left to go to war. The suppressed weeping of the well-heeled, diamond-decked bourgeoisie hung over the auditorium well after the aria was over like a black Hebridean sky struggling to contain its load.

Immigration has also had an impact and, according to some, has intensified this cultural peculiarity, resulting in stereotyping. Faced by a dominant foreign culture, the mother is the sole keeper of the traditions of the old country, the 'incomparably loving, servant and owner of her children, often tearful but always on her feet, holding the family together; adored, feared, strong, dedicating herself to her son intensively'. Whether the phenomenon is more or less than it was, whether it is a more visible, quantifiable passion affecting southern Italians compared to others in the rest of the country, I cannot say. But I do know that both in Italy and within the Italian-Scots community, men will abandon their wives for hours even days at a time to be with their mothers, the *mammissima* (supermamma) as she came to be in an alien country.

While the Rossi and Coletta women were, in my eyes, unparalleled as pioneers for womanhood, the feminist movements of the seventies passed me by. Apart from my mother's inexplicable cowering when confronted by her brother which made me rage at the indignity of it, and my father's ill treatment of her, my aunt Louise and my grandmother, there had been no war to win. I am not sure if their taking control was a natural character trait or if it was more about filling the gap, compensating for their menfolk. The males in my family were, apart from Rico, weak men, though demanding in almost every way, and quite disrespectful of their wives. Despite their unwillingness to work hard, their tendency to linger and joust with cronies, they saw in their masculine role a right to control and even chastise their wives. Card games and golf in the guise of business were how they executed their family duties and they were generally content to rely on the hard work of their wives, both in the home and in the family business, and enjoy the benefits of their long, gruelling hours.

Where both my experience and my understanding of life has been about sensitivity to intimate relationships, about the joys, thrill and excitement, the sadness and disappointments that we sadly often suffer and visit on others, of constant self-interrogation, I saw in those women an apparent total lack of concern about the quality of their marital relationship; a hardy pragmatism about their weaknesses; a tolerance of their men's indulgences – gambling, alcohol and sometimes other women. It was all overlooked, as if how their husbands spent their evenings and nights did not interfere with their role as a business partner. As long as they could put on a clean shirt and a Missoni tie, and usher in regulars to the café, play hardball with the tobacco salesman or negotiate a loan with the bank manager, all was well. Home, too, was merely fabric, for they were not primarily home-makers. Home was simply a place to showcase success and financial prosperity; opulence above taste; no Victorian butter dishes, boot scrapers or Georgian tables here, only Capodimonte, camp statuary and gaudy glassware; bricks and plaster, and lacking the echoes of conversation, banter or song and a family at play.

The pre-eminence of a business role of the women in my family was poorly matched by an interest or ability to mother, the duties of which were disposed of on a sort of needs analysis basis. Consistent with reported social patterns, certainly in the South of Italy, the Italian norm regarding mother and son undoubtedly prevailed in my home.

There was an intensity between Grandma and Rico which I remember very vividly and which disturbed me. His energy was all towards his mother, especially as she got older and less strong, his marital relationship, by contrast, an accommodation in which my aunt hardly figured. My grandmother called her son's wife *na serpe,* a serpent, possibly not directly to him but certainly to us, and their relationship was never warm. Rico visited his mother every day, spending his time away from his shop, taking her into the countryside for afternoon tea. If he did not appear, she would demand to know why, and on one occasion she claimed, bizarrely, since she had no loyalty whatsoever to poor Winnie, his faint wife, that she had seen him in his car with another woman. She was without a doubt close to her son. But the tenor of their relating was conspiratorial rather than loving and tender. In fact, I never saw them embrace. In the years after the war and well into the sixties, our position in Scotland was still uncertain, our survival not quite secure, so he was her *consigliere*, her counsellor, and possibly she his. So they talked mainly business, or how best to harness my mother. There was, there exists in all Italian families in business in Scotland, I think, the constant threat of business 'competition'. Yet when I walk through the streets of Bruntsfield or Broughton Street popular with young professional and alternative Edinburgh, I see at least ten shops where I can buy a coffee, all co-existing, all presumably profitable. But I remember the family outrage when the Falcon Restaurant opened up about two hundred yards from our café in the early sixties. There were continual forays mainly by my grandmother to *fa la spia,* spy, find out how many customers and which of our regulars – the infidels, were in that place and not ours. If Grandma met the owner by chance, she would give him an angry, crushing look, as good as a curse on him and his seed, for he was quite definitely the enemy.

Grandma's death was a tragedy for her son. It left him totally bereft and disorientated, emotionally unstuck, and led him to various religious excesses including an obsession with Padre Pio, resulting in frequent visits to San Giovanni Rotondo, the saint's birthplace. Having been a typical Italian man, leaving all religious observance to the womenfolk as is still common in Italy, he became quite fanatical after her death. He started the habit of Sunday Mass, no matter how busy the shop was, surrounded himself with all manner of blessed rosaries and waters, relics and bits of cloth, teeth, bone chips etc., began to believe in the smell of roses to signal the miraculous presence of the Saint, and was wide-eyed at such unlikely tales as the blessed monk appearing at the window of a plane in flight, holding it aloft when weather was stormy.

My mother, on the other hand, reacted quite differently to her mother's death. She was pragmatic, thoughtful, and I suspect she saw it as her liberation. She had a strong affinity with and terror of the supernatural, rather like her own mother. Indeed, not long before my mother died she was in bed reading one night and suddenly saw her sister, who had died many years since, sitting smiling, young and radiant, at the foot of her bed. My mother did actually agree to accompany my uncle and Winnie on one of these pilgrimages to San Giovanni. But she went only once, never again, and was so overcome with irrational fears in the *pensione* where they stayed, in the church when the Padre said Mass, and at the sight of him, his bandaged hands (for he was known to have the 'stigmata', a curious phenomenon) on the other side of the open confessional box, that she could not be left alone for fear of a night visitation; and poor Winnie had to desert her marital bed to share with my mother. This probably pleased her more than she would say, since Winnie was none too enthusiastic about Rico and his pursuit of 'nonsense'!

The mother-son bond apart, *mammismo* as it was played out in my home, was virulent and even toxic. My grandmother was very different towards her daughters. Motherhood towards them was more a biographical detail rather than a role. It had little day-to-day reality. It is possible that her inability to be active in business as she got older, her enforced withdrawal into the home and the subsequent distress caused, affected Grandma's ability to show care. I saw no warmth or tender contact between her and my mother or Louise.

My grandmother, though she looked after me well and

sowed seeds that yielded richly, did not mother willingly. If she did feel any visceral connection with her children, it was superseded by her need to be in the public eye and successful. Of her six grandchildren, only one had more than one child. I have pondered over the reasons for this pervading family reticence to parent prolifically. The joylessness that was a feature of our childhood as cousins I believe, still lingered on. The issue of livelihood and survival in a country that saw us as interlopers remained. And the business of marriage and children was ultimately as it had originally been in an Italian village which none of us had ever visited, a practical one, for those were the lessons we had learned, this was how we understood life. The upbringing of children was not an end in itself, it was not considerate or sensitive; the rough rearing of us and subsequently of the next generation was adapted to shop life and the practicalities of its requirements. I remember when the good Winnie, chosen months before to be my Confirmation sponsor, telephoned as we were leaving the house, me at the age of nine in my sacramental white, to tell us she was unable to come because the café was busy, thereby reducing my desperate mother to appealing to the crowd of parents gathered at the convent chapel for a sponsor, so that I could go through with the ceremony. And then there was the terrible scene between my mother and Grandma on the night of the school concert, the impact of it, when I was due to perform a solo piano piece and several two piano pieces with my close friend Kathleen. I was sick with nerves, but I was even sicker at the extreme violence of my grandmother throwing open all the windows of the house, calling for an end to her life and banging her head on her bedroom wall. So bitter was the exchange between her and my mother that my own distress was unheeded by both.

My asthma was due, I think, to the levels of tension and anger which surrounded me; from the last years of my mother's marriage to her frequent confrontations with her own mother. I was in bed so often that my life and development were disrupted. I believe that experience has influenced much of the way I have chosen to live my life since. I become claustrophobic and intolerant if I am held back or contained. Unwilling to be tied down by partners or people except my own children, I have a sense of exploration, never routines or habits, trying new things, noting interest, moving on. I experiment with new identities, a series of masks and faces, presentations of a central me. I live life with an excitement and optimism, as if it will be snatched away and I will not have tomorrow. I was so tired of spending endless lonely days in bed, as far back as I can recall, that I learned from early on to pretend that I was well. I tried at all costs to overcome my feeling of inability to breathe, that weakness in my legs, that sluggishness and lethargy that comes when your lungs are full. If I could work through it, show no weakness to my mother and grandmother, I was sure that unnoticed, the unbidden ailment would go away. One morning I remember being dressed in my school uniform, feeling weak and breathless. My mother and I were standing at the door. As she opened it for us to leave, she looked at me and said, 'You're not well, are you?' 'No,' I said. The feeling of relief at being found out, of surrender and the beating of my mother's heart as I laid my head against it, is a memory I return to often, with a longing for that one moment of laying myself down that can never go away.

My mother made up for her physical awkwardness with me, for her thoughtlessness, her unwillingness to engage in conversation beyond the racy, to ferret out or share truths, by being a wonderful grandmother to my three daughters. She was loving, fun and mostly funny. She delighted in them; swelled with pride at them. They have many tales of their own about her, but the funniest for me was the day that she collected them from school in a taxi and it was raining. A woman approached her with her own children, who attended the same school and asked to share the taxi. Unfazed, without paying the slightest attention to the request, my mother went on into the taxi, gathering the girls to her, all the while muttering to them under her breath, 'I'm pretending I'm deaf.' Then she closed the door, sat back contentedly and sailed off. She gave a lot of her time to her three grandchildren, whom she often looked after when my husband and I were at work in our busy careers. It was she who taught them to read before they began school, shared her ability to draw with them, nursed them if they were ill. When she had her clothes shop, she kept them with her in the back with her dog, feeding him leftover spaghetti and them fried egg rolls and Digestive biscuits buttered both sides. She made no secret of the fact that she was under pressure from my father to have a child and that it was not her choice to have me. She often blamed me for the failure of her marriage, because I was too demanding, too often ill.

It was because of me she often said, that she was not able to remarry being maybe wisely unwilling to bring another man, this time not my father, into the family home. She did come to love me, though, was openly proud of me, admiring even; she boasted annoyingly, I imagine, about my ability at school, my career, my homemaking and how I looked. She even sent me down the catwalk as a warm-up to her fashion shows. I have been many things, but never a model, nonetheless I rather happily obliged. I was in fact delighted to pose for photographs for the Edinburgh local newspaper wearing some new season's pieces from my mother's shop. I did eventually come to find The Copper Kettle intriguing as a teenager, but as a youngster, I longed for a home life, a meal cooked for me rather than having to rustle up yet another steak in the back shop, eating in the café seated alone in that wee staff corner, observed, and sometimes interrupted, when I just wanted to eat quietly.

While I was equally proud of my mother's dramatic looks

and spirit of enterprise, her wide literary and artistic interests unlike those of her community, I was very much in need
of closeness with her, but I could never say it, not really even
to myself. I just had a deep sense of void, a malaise, things
not quite complete. Somehow with her it was hard to say
loving words. She was rarely open to connecting in that way,
brushing things off with flippancy and humour. I wanted her
warmth, her smell, the evenness of her quiet breathing, just
now and again. If I really wanted a cuddle, even as a grown
woman, I would climb on her knee until she, amused and
embarrassed would tell me to get off because I was too big.
After another disastrous night when I crept into the house
late and sat defeated on my bed following a self-destructive
disco, when I was afraid of the dark and wandered into her
bed for comfort, or when I was crippled with an anxiety that
nuclear war might break out, or that a balcony would suddenly give way in the King's Theatre, I craved her complete
attention. I wanted her to show me who she really was and
what she really felt, to reach out and put her finger on what
lay behind my masquerade of being even and in control. I
wanted her not to tell me to get back to my own bed, but to
enjoy the honest cradling, the natural seamlessness and that
unspoken draw always, of a mother to her child.

Who I am as a mother is not something I have learned
from my Italian upbringing and nor is it something that I
have copied from my Scottish friends. I certainly did not
want to be a part of the norms, circles, roles and behaviours
of the Scottish mothers around me, with whom I had little in
common; who flocked and nattered and were concerned with
the daily trivia of life; who as far as I could see, were content
to retire into domesticity and caring, and to be reliant on
their men. For I was, at that stage of my life, a professional
woman, bred otherwise, differently female, moving forward
with a career, ambition and self-made opportunity. Nor did
I find any role models of motherhood in the Scottish Italian

community which, at a personal level and increasingly together with my family, I had almost totally deserted, for in this new found environment of mine, more liberal, cultured and refined, I had little in common with them. I did though partly because of my husband and partly because of my professional role, a teacher of languages including Italian, revisit that community from time to time, his community, a different community and not mine. I have some memories of uncomfortable, dispiriting weddings and christenings, not on the dance floor but in back rooms, for that was where the women lodged, which overwhelmed me with the same hopelessness of my past. While my husband was fêted and lauded as a solicitor by the Italian businessmen of the community, anxious to impress or indeed seek advice, I, young, vibrant and yes, sexy, stoically endured the accounts of matronly complaints about menopause, swollen ankles and family ills. My one dear wish was actually to join the men or dance away the menacing blues. In my Scottish middle class environment, therefore, I was Italian. Whilst in the community of my past, I was *Scocces*... 'Scotch' and therefore a migrant in both. Sadly, in brief conversation over one of the standard twelve celebratory dinner courses, followed a few hours later by giant panini stuffed with hams and provolone cheese, surrounded by large women wearing black, by men smiling too broadly, by backslapping and bonhomie, my dialect belying my bearing, the dejected image of me, *la moglie dell' avvocato,* lawyer's wife, that was reflected back, told me that I had not travelled far at all.

I had a fine lineage of strong successful women, active, directional and creative, which had positioned me well for my path in life. But as a prospective new mother, I had as my abstract ideal of mothering, my strong sense of what I needed as a child and didn't get; my need for exclusivity, my need to see joy in the watching and hearing of me, interest in my progress, my growing skills and aptitudes; my need to be delighted in, to see sparkle, to be brought in from the skirting board from where I knew I had to be mute and invisible to the warm centre of family life; and a need to know that whatever the failings, the mistakes, the dilemmas, no matter how enormous the fall, however far from the ideal, a loving, restoring and accepting hand would hold mine and there would always be a breast to lay my head on; a place to run to where I could believe that I was, am, and will always be beautiful and good. While others fussed about night feeds, green stools and the paraphernalia of baby care, this ideal is what drove me as a first time mother.

I did not set out to change the norms of the one-child family, though I did. I did seek to banish forever my home culture and the destructiveness of that environment; I did seek to reverse the paradigm, and I did. And as my three girls, Camilla, Roberta and Sophie-Louise grew and even as my career took me here, there and everywhere, I increasingly wanted to be the *mammissima*, 'incomparably loving', the centre of the family, the holder of legacy and tradition, uniquely placed as the years pass, to hand traditions on. It is for them to judge if I am on course for success, for parenting is a lifelong journey of learning. I am in no doubt that as their mother I have made other serious mistakes, left them wanting, been absent or distracted when I should have been present. But with my three daughters, these inspiring women in whose company I now live my life, I took the final step towards freedom from the black years; I was able to replace my own family background with the positive, loving one in the home that I and my husband created. For he played his part fulsomely. So, to the astonishment of my family and mostly my mother, I embarked on a journey of homemaking, mothering and career. To the entrepreneurship, the hard-headed manoeuvring and instinct for business success I had so admired in the women who brought me up, to the progress that they made, the foundations that they laid, I added the deep, instinctive, visceral bonds of being a mother to my girls. While like those before me, I worked hard with the same ambition and dedication, I never held back from energetically creating a home for my children, where our friends and theirs were welcome. I believe I did not fail, whatever my defaulting, in building a strong family life of fun, food and ever love.

Through motherhood I found all the healing for the damage of my upbringing. While I created context, it was my daughters who lived within and peopled that context: gardens and bicycles; cartoons, birthday parties and barbecues; the Singing Kettle and Michael Jackson; recorders, cellos and pianos; Christmas Eve parties; picnics, fireworks and fairy tales; nursery rhymes, poems and story books; kitchen table and fireside. My daughters were quite simply the personalities that they were. Together we, my husband and I, and they, created something that had eluded me, that I had only heard of, observed but never experienced. While my girls delighted in them, for me too they were a first experience. The novelty of family, fun, the natural urge to always place your loveable children at the centre of everything and to please them was incontrovertible, never in question. It has left me wondering how in my own family of passionate Italian mothers it was otherwise. For it was joy that we, my children and I, gave and continue to give to each other; joy at their childishness, at gumminess, at lisping, at morning dreaminess and sleepiness, at tunelessness, at the warmth of small and less small bodies, at dimpled knees, at unreasonableness, at wonder, at the smell of skin and scalp, at licking plates and grabbing at prawns and drumsticks. At drooling over pasta and love of pizza. The sight of a blond, almost one-year-old trying to stay upright in a Tuscan garden and shouting 'happy' will remain forever with me. The question of 'how do you know when God is smiling?' from a four-year-old at six in the morning will not leave me. And the outraged demand from my eldest

daughter – 'Mummy carry you' – in clammy Florida was
only yesterday, though thirty-seven years have gone by. I
had no idea how to be a mother, my daughters taught me.
I had few expectations of motherhood, my children taught
me the wonders and adventures of it. I had no childhood,
my children gave me one. While I had carried sadness and
loneliness, my children gave me friendship and family. While
I had longed for intimacy, my children demanded my knee,
my kisses and even my bed and my bath at times that suited
them and often not me. And the wonder of morning waking,
beside a soft, innocent, sleeping child or the trusting nestling
of a troubled teenager at the end of a hard school day, my
grown daughter's head seeking rest on my shoulder through
a relationship break-up or the loss of a job, these are truly
precious moments. It was these things, lifetime rooting, they
to me and I to them, that we lovingly, unreservedly gave and
go on giving.

To my role of mother, I also brought a way of thinking
about food which was certainly foreign to my experience of
Scottish life, which was neither considered nor observed, but
arrived at and instinctive. I had been to many gatherings in
friends' homes, I had seen soufflés and sophistication, truffles
and tortes, at-homes and blow-outs. I had eaten venison and
vol-au-vents. But as a child, I had learned from Grandma
the importance of food as love, food as communication and
communion; the kitchen table as the centre of the home; and
I had learned the cheering, warming welcome of abundance
and simplicity; of overburdened tables and over-full fridges,
of unaffected, unselfconscious presentations, and of the
importance for family of food as ceremony. I had seen
the miracle of homemaking through the *coufidou*, a two-
day beef stew of l'Aveyron in France, and the thick hearty
apricot jams of Madame Froment, Marie-Cécile's mother,
both businesswoman and *mère de famille*; and I had tasted
the wonderful pastas and gnocchi, oxtails and rich soups of

my wonderful Aunt Louise, the heart of both business and home and the strength of her family, who had died far too soon. None of these women sacrificed how and what they fed their family, how they brought their family together.

Grandma insisted on celebration, at Easter particularly, with *frittatas*, ritualistic lemons and the baking of savouries I am even unable to spell; puff pastries encasing nutty prosciuttos. The Froment family gathered each night to eat five-course dinners with wine and good conversation. Aunt Louise cooked each night every time my mother and I, later I alone, visited. I learned from these business baronesses that food is never about compromise; that food and family are one and the same; that no matter what the day or the stresses or the demands, what satisfies, what sustains, what truly nourishes is the simple delight of fresh food. I learned it in France, I saw it for myself in Milan, Bologna, Tuscany and Puglia; I learned it in Spain, Portugal and in Asia. If I did see a sandwich for dinner, it was either for tourists on a shoestring or made with ingredients, colourful, fragrant, cooked with a care, adorned with crisp leafy greenery, that made me dribble. While I too, like these empresses of their kitchens, bore the burdens of budgets, bullying, long hours and competition that make up serious professional life as well as shop life, I have never, would never eat a ready meal, a frozen pizza or put either in front of my family. I love them, value food and indeed my wonderful Italian heritage too much.

As ethnically Italian, I sought to be the *mammissima* and in the end I found it impossible to be otherwise. I am and have always been physically and emotionally passionate about and to my children. I have of course seen the negative effects of *mammismo* and possessiveness, of ownership of children by parents, the destroying of lives as a result of it; lives hardly lived, days spent as remnants of the forcefulness of what was; and confronted early on the possibility of the ruination of mine, had I not left family and community behind. However, while I am able to stand back, give way to partners, not direct, restraint where my children are concerned is an impossibility. If I want to overwhelm my twenty-eight-year-old daughter with kisses, I will not hold back despite any partner who observes us. If I want to cradle the head of my thirty-six-year-old, I will do it tenderly anywhere and at any time. If I want to cuddle up to my thirty year old in a hotel bed, nothing will stop me. Equally, if I feel I am being blocked or shut out emotionally, I will say so, I will challenge and assert my rights as a mother to follow my children's development and journey; my rights, in the absence of better, to care; and my ultimate duty, responsibility and will, when all other fails, to make things right.

There has been a mixed journey of progress and ascent throughout this account of my life, with some backward glances, some lingering emotional clinging and some inescapable imprints of nature and birthright. The route up and out to a kind of levelling has not been chronological. Rather, it has been arranged in order of importance, in order of what liberated and made me who I am today, late in my life. As in Dante's glorious finale, I believe that I have kept the best, the most profound experience of moulding, of discovery and finding the lost ark that passed me by in my early years, to the last. I am referring of course to all that my daughters have given to me, for I lived their growing-up with them, gave them what I had never had, often improvised, that sense of being loveable, able to do whatever they wanted to undertake. I sat on swings with them, bumped my way down chutes in park playgrounds, did undignified congas with them in night clubs, got on the table in a Hard Rock café while they tried to pull me down, steered a barge in France topless while they crouched in embarrassment, and basically found the carefree and the child in me. But mostly, I found a love that I never thought I would earn or feel. For all of this, I thank them for saving me.

Footlights

Concluding Thoughts

THERE ARE THREE things you need to know about pasta. Firstly, you must treat it as an honoured guest at your table. Like the humble haggis, which is traditionally piped in and addressed at some length, simple pasta requires ceremony. Secondly, in order to merit its prime position at the head of the table, for it is always dished up there by the cook and handed around, it should be if served in a *ragù*, coated lightly in the sauce to give it colour, and then the final glorious topping of rich tomato piled high. This crowning marks its arrival. Make sure that your pasta is white, never wholemeal, it should be an egg pasta, for it partners sauces best and will glisten and glow most fetchingly as you approach your fork. The *ragù* should contain a few tablespoonfuls of the water the pasta was cooked in and there should be enough *ragù* left for diners to add according to their taste. Pasta is for us, the queen of meals. One third and final piece of advice, apart from a prohibition on knives (never cut pasta) – when a plate of pasta is put in front of you, cooked in the way that I have described, eat it joyously, without restraint and certainly not as if you don't really want it, which is often what I observe among over polite non Italians! Sucking, slurping are in this context acceptable. Gobbling is a sign of excellence. Second, third and dare I say, fourth helpings, a clean plate and sauce stains on your clothing are the hallmarks of pleasure and the greatest compliment to any cook. While I began this book with a description about my complicated relationship with milk, probably cultural, my relationship with pasta has never faltered. Not once. In all its moods, its colour bold, an operatic triumph or its aura comforting and subdued, a Goldberg Variation, pasta has been with me from childhood. From those first beginnings, the rich fragrance of Sunday in Morningside, in Bruntsfield with Grandma, in The Copper Kettle with my mother and Ernestina, waiting for a lull in business to put a key in the door and attack; and ultimately in my own family home with husband and children, excitement in the chatter, doorbell ringing, a fall off a bike, when I have tried hard to honour a fine legacy at Easter and at Christmas time, pasta has been my link to home and a tradition I want to keep and share.

*

I vividly remember two particular books I used to read to my youngest daughter Sophie- Louise. One was *Mog in the Dark* by Judith Kerr. It is an enchanting book about the eponymous cat Mog who cannot get into the house where she lives and ends up somewhat pathetically on the rooftops watching her family together in the house but is unable to join them. The other was Sam McBratney's timeless story *Guess How Much I Love You*. Through this piece of work I wanted my daughters to know who their mother is, for I never had that level of honesty with mine. I wonder whether the events of the war, the sudden loss of her father, the living with all that my father brought, and regrets about her decision to marry him had been of such proportions that it was easier to hide in laughter. But I regret not finding the ways to reach her, I regret the masks. In telling my daughters a final, grown up story, sharing my history, I want to give them a sense of belonging, rooting and homecoming. I want to gift these to the women that I have helped to create with love, this testament which they and those that follow them might return to again and again throughout their lives, wherever they are.

*

Of the many strands in this book, my relationship with my mother is central and complex. There was jealousy and resentment, competitiveness and shared pride one for the other, disapproval together with fierce love. Mainly there was humour though and my best memories are laughing with her. No one since, except my eldest daughter, Camilla, has ever made me laugh more. There were many times too when our roles reversed, times when she needed to be rescued, when she made wrong decisions, and times when my tenderness at her wide-eyed trust either reduced my speech to gruff monosyllables or choked off any words. But there were times too when I rejoiced in her daring and her ferocity. It stirred my own. I have been harsh on her mothering I realise, and she could have launched me better into the world with a stronger sense of being fine just as I am, instead of my continual need to feel accepted and to be universally liked and loved. But I now know, with the new insights and perspectives that writing this book has given me, that hers was an even greater struggle to find her identity than mine has been. For she lived in times that favoured women and Italians even less than in my own era. As a woman who had a strong sense of what she wanted for herself, her years were dominated by a constant search for love and romance, for security; maybe in fact we are not as dissimilar as I have thought, for she was mothered no better than I was.

*

I want to pay tribute to the women who went before me, all of them restless, striving, strident, never relegated or

199

put aside. For on the road to getting established, to getting us Italian women established and visible, they continually confronted and challenged. Not one stood still. Acceptance and small attainable horizons do not come easily to our kind. Where one left off, another picked up. Grandma, barely able to write her name, travelled from Leith Walk, and with the panache that she eventually developed, took possession of the lobby of a Hydro Hotel in the Scottish Borders, ordered afternoon tea, learned that ritual. Auntie Louise, her lips always hurriedly etched in red while she rode her morning taxi to work and to manage, after some quick banter with her neighbour, Louis in the backyard, the Italians in the ice cream factory at the side of her house in Victory Road, threw on her mink, strode out to lunch with the wife of the Lord Mayor, and replaced that dialect, Collaluca and Coletta, with the sweetly diffident city smile of hers. My mother could grab a man by the tie if he threatened her day's takings, reduce a cigarette traveller to a quiver and when facing a lawsuit once, for a customer sadly fell into our cellar, she sweetened the judge with the words of our language. Grabbing the headlines in the local paper, she turned misfortune to advantage, resumed her laughing self, and emerged cheery at the increase in coffee sales. Equally, she commanded the best gin and tonics in town in the five star Edinburgh George Hotel, wore a range of knitwear of the highest quality, was known at every cosmetic counter in Princes Street, drank coffee among the fashionistas of Jenners tearoom and the ladies of Fullers; and in one of the most exclusive restaurants in the capital, followed her smoked salmon with a request to the head waiter for a soup plate and a tasting selection of all the deserts on the trolley.

Each of us has built on the victories and survival of the other. We emerged from a past in order that I was able eventually to cross a boundary, travelling from my background of frothy coffee and chips and merging, though not without distress at times, into the middle classes. For in relation to class, Italian Scots were unassigned. I have left upper-class balls desperate for a wild Highland fling and middle-class dinner parties frustrated at gentility, desperate for a fish supper. Or better... *na buona magnad...* a good feed. That is dinner. It is my love of great music and the arts and not social convention or expectations which take me to concerts, the opera and art galleries. From there, I blended into a professional way of life, trimmed my sails, practised quiet containment. At the top end of that career, both my gender and my ethnicity were foreign but in grappling with that, embracing the ways of a native Scot, often my guard slipping, we, I forged an environment from which my children could start their own journey on new and equal terms with those around them. We levelled the field. For not one of us before my daughters' generation started out as peers on Scottish soil. That honour had to be earned and worked at.

*

This story of mine is a song of victory and I sing it loudly. It demonstrates the power of aspiration, the power of imagination and determination; sunshine over shadow, self over circumstance. Arrival. But still, unlike my daughters, totally adapted and integrated, I am the constant traveller, a migrant. I have lived my life between cultures, Italian and Scottish. At different stages of my life, I have been more Italian and at others more Scottish. My Scottishness obtrudes when in Viticuso or Milan, my *italianismo* bulges in Perth or Pitlochry, in Board rooms and in places where music and poetry flourish. In Florence someone once asked how many years I had lived abroad. I have never fully taken up residence anywhere or in any milieu, even when I wanted to. That betweenness, that no man's land is my enduring legacy from my background. That neutral space is also somewhere from where I can observe both worlds. It is a place I can withdraw to, make decisions from, a larger space opened up with many more options. And what a much richer life experience somehow, not to fit. How much more is available to you when you connect only in part; and it is absolutely the part which jars, the critical eye on what is before and behind you but mainly on self, which is the one that takes you to a new place, new people and some clear, new understanding and articulation of who you are.

*

My relationship with Italy will always be complex, my feelings for it volatile, contradictory. But whatever my feelings on any particular day or at any stage in my life, they are always absolutely, incontrovertibly and passionately proud and protective, irritated and embarrassed or plainly amused. When I say that I love Italy, I do not mean that I feel tender or tearful but more a raw, spontaneous sense of consummation and satisfaction. I fall into the rich low tones of the southern tongue and I feel my blood rise. I watch old people in a market, in church, sitting on a park bench chatting, I want to talk, to listen, to hold a hand for they remind me of my grandmother. I listen to a Vivaldi quartet in a cloister in Tuscany, see the finesse of a tailored businessman in a Milan bar, am caught up at the sight of a group at a white tableclothed lunch, the ooze of soft polenta and a glass of Vernaccia di San Gimignano in a trattoria in Mantova. I am gladdened by wisdom, by bent fingers, by old, lined faces browned by the sun, by the elegance of appearance and gait, by such evident animated pleasure in food, people and life itself. These aspects of my birthright, together with those processions with Madonnas adorned in Euros, wedding dresses, whole heads of hair and gold chains in the sacristy of a small local church; the affected learnedness of a parish priest; that continental shrug of the shoulder; the knowing glint in the eye of a waiter when he has overcharged you or not come back with your change; those raised voices; the barking dogs in the early hours; the sweep of an azure coastline bathed in a heartening sun; the brightly coloured cruising cars; pompous policemen; early morning, looking down on Florence, a Romanesque church at your back; this is my Italy.

*

And so I am the end of my story. Elena Ferrante was my inspiration, for what I took from her among many things was the courage to describe a reality and a stark truthfulness. I recognise in myself as in her main character a persistent inability to let go; a reluctance to fully inhabit any chosen persona, world or language; and from time to time, a tendency to walk backwards; to be in continual motion. Ever the migrant that I am, it is I believe from the spaces between identities, cultures and difference that new language is born.

In Boat of Garten near Loch Garten in the Cairngorm mountains of Scotland, there is a nest and breeding area for the osprey, which for some time has been threatened by extinction. Some of the birds reared there return year after year after a brief period of migration to West Africa. Others never return. Some die. Scotland, the chosen fresh ground of my Italian grandparents, is where through a troubled beginning for all of us... I have built my own nest. Through the history of years here, the feet that I followed, the voices I grew from, the hands that I held and that held mine, those that I didn't dare to hold and those I can no longer hold, the faces that I cherish and love, it is this Scotland that I willingly, wholeheartedly own. While I gaze at times across to other distant landscapes, Italy and beyond, it is in this Scotland, these waters, these islands; these places of liberal education and intellectual freedoms; these coffee shops, eateries, and clothes shops; these hostels and hotels that I have chosen to be. For it is the sturdy, honest, loyal heart of it, the energy and vigorous independence of spirit of it, the openness and genuineness of its good, good people that make me finally able to say, I am happily and profoundly rooted and from where my daughters, Camilla, Roberta and Sophie-Louise have freely and magnificently owned the skies.

Love Songs

Benedetto sia 'l giorno, et 'l mese, et l'anno,
e la stagione, e 'l tempo, et l'ora, e 'l punto,
e 'l bel paese, e 'l loco ov'io fui giunto
da'duo begli occhi che legato m'hanno
(Petrarch, Il Canzoniere)

One

Her Facebook voice sings deep in me
I still make her rice pudding.
The answers to my daughters' questions
long grown all
are still the same
…yes I am your mummy
yes, I love you this much
yes, I love you to the sky and back again…

And yes, I will carry you.

Two

Why don't you come and sit over here?
(I love you)

Can I get you a cup of tea?
(I will always love you)

Do you want to talk about it?
(You stop my heart)

I'll give you a call later
(I love every hair on your head)

How's life been?
(I love you over and over)

Ok then... just leave
(I am nothing without you)

I am going away for a bit
(I love you, why are we fighting?)

Can I do that for you?
(There's a crumb on your cheek)

Will you please stop moving about..
(Coorie doun sweetheart)

Will we eat this at the table?
(Sunshine in your eyes)

Three

My friend let me warm you.
How long have you been sitting here?
Will we walk maybe?
Can you come now?

Four

That voice that still says *never give up, stand still*
that phone call that says *yes*
the small bird that took me down a Perthshire mountain
One Sunday in snow
was and is my mother.

Five

Loving…

a Commedia of words…

lone litanies…

sand through your fingers…

Petrarca's blessings…

always finding the one…

whose smell brings you home.

Melody in Minor Key

It's all in the key you see
and oh the chill blue of that particular one
catching us all unawares
no resting here that's clear
and that's why I will take it with me
no pictures, for their faces are written on my own
no lock of daughters' hair
for the strands of our days together will ever bind me.

No its the sheet of music I mean
when I go
and I will go
notes flattened to ease my passage
tease me onwards
for I don't really belong here with them nor with you
I will pick up that same old tune to guide me
as I have over and over again
I will fill every one of my pockets with it
fade away again into something major
bold again
for a while anyway.

Viticusar

The Language of Viticuso and Thereabouts

THROUGHOUT THIS ACCOUNT, I have used *viticusar*, an Italian which I learned as a first language from my grandmother. I have tried to give some sense of the distinct character of that dialect, the sound and music of it; its sayings, wisdoms and humour that is an essential element of it and of its people. I have listed here below, the words used in the book, as well as some of the sayings and other words or phrases that are so familiar to the people here in Scotland and also in *Gl' Vitratur* (Viticuso) with whom I share the same origins.

As far as I know, the language does not exist in written form and will probably, like my generation, in time become obsolete. I have wanted for many years to find a means of recording, setting down somewhere, this loveable, eccentric language. There is a kind of reluctance now to own and speak it and so I am taking this opportunity to give this aspect of our rich heritage a place and a voice.

The list is random, from memories of childhood and by no means exhaustive. My hope would be that my daughters come to fully appreciate and value it as their language too; and that in making it visible, I might open the way for contributions from other sources, begin a dialogue and create in a very small way, a means of keeping the language alive.

For the purposes of understanding, in the following pages the *viticusar* dialect is presented first, followed by the Italian in brackets, then literal translation, then the meaning, as appropriate. This order is not followed if the translation is straightforward. For some words and phrases there is no direct translation. These are followed simply by an explanation. Gesture is required for some of the phrases. Any inconsistencies in this section are a reflection of the nature of a spoken, rather than written, language.

(*la*) *ballarella*: old village dance involving a handkerchief between the couple to avoid touch

(*gle*) *baston* (*il bastone*): the stick or rod of discipline
GESTURE – with an open right hand, making a cutting motion at an angle.

('*na*) *buon sfogad'* (*una buona sfogata*): getting things off your chest

bracciol (*braccioli*): beef olives

che può fa? (*che cosa si può fare?*): what can you do?
GESTURE – shrug of the shoulders, hands upturned

chiam' a Di' ch' c'aiud (*chiediamo l'aiuto di Dio*): let's call on God's help; may God help us now

chill' beglie padan 're Viticus' (*quelle belle patate di Viticuso*): those wonderful potatoes from Viticuso

chi me vuò cott' e chi me vuò crur (*chi mi vuole cotto e chi mi vuole crudo*): some want me cooked and some want me raw; I'm overwhelmed

chi pecore se fa, gle lup' se la magne (*chi pecora si fa, il lupo se la mangia*): act the sheep and the wolf will eat you; stand up for yourself

chi si tu? (*tu chi sei?*): who are you?

GESTURE – shake of the hand which is upturned and fingers bunched together

chi spud nell' aria, gle reve n' facce (*chi sputa nell'aria gli riviene in faccia*): if you spit in the air, it comes right back on your face; don't make trouble

('na) ciociar' (*una ciociara*): southern Italian woman; woman from *La Ciociaría*

co' du per renda na scarp' (*con tutt'e due i piedi in una scarpa*): with two feet in one shoe; timidly

(ne) cornud (*un cornudo*): womaniser

cott' pe n'om (*cotta per un uomo*): hot for a man; wanting to get laid

Di' lavor' in n'or (*Dio lavora in un ora*): God works in an hour; an act of God

è menud co' 'na man innanz e un adredd (*è venuto con una mano davanti e una indietro*): s/he arrived with one hand covering the front and the other his/her backside; to come empty handed.

è menud man vacand (*è venuto senza niente in mano*): s/he came empty handed

fa ben e scordate, fa mal e pensace (*fa bene e scordati, fa male e pensaci*): forget the good that you do and reflect on the wrongs

('na) facenner (*donna iperattiva*): hyperactive woman; busybody

faglie la spes' (*fagli le spese*): buy what they offer; learn from others (*'ne) fesse (uno stupido)*: stupid or gullible person

fa figur; (*fare figura, figura*): put on a good show or present well; keep up appearances

fa la spi' (*fare la spia*): to spy on someone

fatte' maestr' mamà (fatti maestra, amore): become a teacher, my love

fa schiv' (*fa schifo*): it or s/he is disgusting; it or s/he makes me sick; it's outrageous (*schifos'* (adj) – bad or disgusting; I 'schiv' that, it makes me sick)

furbezz' (*furbezza*): cunning
GESTURE – with right-hand index finger, pull at the skin under the right eye

gnor Zi' (*lo zio Monsignore*): uncle the Monsignor exalted rank in the Roman Catholic clergy

iam' n cul alla legge (*ce ne frega la legge*): up the arse of the law; to hell with the law

(*'na) lamentos (una lamentosa)*: moaning woman; a moaner

(*'ne) maestre (un professore)*: teacher

(*gle) mal' oiche (il mal occhio)*: the evil eye (southern Italian superstition)

Mammà, mamà (cara, amore): dear darling (intimate term of endearment to a child)
(*'Mammà Mia Dammi Cento Lire'* is a well known song of emigration to America; Mamma without the accented 'a' means mother)

marocchinate: a war crime committed by Les Goumiers in World War two, French Moroccan auxiliaries; to be 'moroccanned'

(la) Marronn (la Madonna): The Virgin Mary

man sciode (le mani sciolte): deft

nella vecchaia le cavze rosse (nella vecchiaia le calze rosse): in old age, red socks; disinhibited old age

nun c'e mette ne sal e ne olio (non ci metto ne sale e ne olio): I won't put salt or oil on the matter; I'm not interfering

nun ce ver cchiù pe la fam' (non ci vedo più per la fame): I'm blind with hunger; I'm beyond starving

pan e cipoll' (pane e cipolli): bread and onions

pe conosce na persona ci ter a magna ne quintal re sal (per conoscere qualcuno bisogna mangiare una tonnellata di sale): you need to eat a ton of salt in order to know someone; you never really know someone

pe mantene' la salud (per mantenere la salute): keep your health up

'na pecore appress a n'om (come una pecora dietro l'uomo) trailing after a man like a sheep; subservient woman

(gle) Piciniscar (il piciniscano): person/language of Picinisco (a village in Lazio)

'na puttan (una puttana): slut

quann' me mor'i (quando io muoio): when I die

ripassà (imitare): mimic

(la) salud (la salute): health

s'a mess mezz 'na via pe si fa mena n'cap (*si è messo in mezzo cercando difficoltá*): stood on the roadway to get hit on the head; he was looking for trouble

s'a mort' Gelardin (*è morto Gelardino*): Gerard has died

(*'na*) *serpe* (*una serpa*): snake

sott' 'na macer (*sotto l'albero*): under a tree

te pozze schiattà (*che ti possa scoppiare*): I hope you burst; a curse on you

te trov alle ball e ter a ballà (*ballo si deve ballare*): when at the dance, you must dance; it's important to fit in

va colla la lun' (*va con la luna*): s/he changes with the moon; s/he is flighty or unpredictable

(*gle*) *Vitratur*
Viticuso, a village in Lazio

vuò mette gle per n'coppe ogni pred (*vuole mettere i pied su ogni sasso*): he wants to put his feet on every stone; he won't leave things be

zi (*zio/zia*): aunt, uncle

Some other choice words and sayings: these are presented randomly

a chi vuò fa fess? (*a chi pensi ingannare*): Who are you trying to fool? GESTURE – right hand upturned and up/down motion, fingers bunched together

addò sem arrivad? (*dove siamo andati a finire*): how have we got to this?

chi se mett' la camice pe la prima vod, se la cag' (*chi si mette la camicia per la prima volta se la caca*): he who puts a shirt on for the first time soils it; don't get above yourself.

chissà addò iam a fini (*chi sa dove andiamo a finire*): who knows where we will end up

magne che te fa rosse (*mangia così cresci*): eat so you'll grow

mo verem' (*adesso vediamo*): we'll soon see

nun me pozze preballe (*Ho perso l'equilibrio*): I need to find my balance

cu la trippe chien (*con lo stomaco pieno*): full belly

chiane, chiane (*piano piano*): slowly does it
GESTURE – right hand slowly revolving

nun me fa n'gazzà (*non mi fare arrabbiare*): don't make me lose my temper

cab toste; teston (*testa dura*): obstinate, hardheaded

aiutete (*sbrigati*): hurry up

nun è buon a niend (*non sa fare niente*): good for nothing

ne schivon (*uno che fa schifo*): a disgusting person

fa fess e contend (*ingannare una persona*): to keep someone in happy ignorance

ne furbacchion (*un furbacchione*): a wily one, a dodger
GESTURE – right hand index finger pull at the skin under the right eye

me fa sci pazz' (mi fa impazzire): he drives me crazy

chuis (lui): he (subject pronoun)

chelle (lei): she (subject pronoun)

esse (lei): her (object pronoun)

n'goppe (sopra): on top

a chi mettess willì (a chi metterebbe voglia): he or she is unattractive

che che facc' (con che faccia): What a cheek

sgarbad (sgarbata): clumsy

sciagurad (sciagurata): tragic woman

na bust' (un corsetto, un busto): a corset

sgustumad (scostumato): immoral or dissolute person

vocca rapert (bocca aperta): indiscreet person

mannegg' (managgia): damn
GESTURE – right hand quick upward movement

Buon alm (buon alma): RIP

scavze e nur e mort re fam (scalzo e nudo e morto di fame): down and out

Ges' Crist' aiutam (Gesú Cristo aiutami): Christ help me

Gesù, Giusepp', Sant Ann' e Marì (Gesù, Giuseppe, Sant'Anna e Maria): Jesus, Mary and Joseph *na spaghettad* (*una spaghettata*): a feast of pasta

na femmine (*una donna*): a woman

meglie sol che mal accumpagnad (*meglio solo che accompagnato male*): better to be alone than to be badly partnered

na mala voglie (*una mala voglia*): an ill will

se De vuò (*se il Dio vuole*): God willing

presuntos (*precoce*): precocious

sfacciad (*sfacciato*): brazen, outspoken

capetost' (*testa dura*): obstinate

a cape sott' (*a testa in giú*): upside down

Two nicknames for fun

scimpe sciampe: someone with a slow, dopey gait

mitt' a quà: exhortation to an inept lover!

Timeline

1913   Maria (Mariuccia) Rossi, neé Coletta, joins her
husband Emilio in Edinburgh. They set up an ice
cream and confectioner's shop in Bonnington Road,
Leith. They live in the back shop.

1917   (January) Cristina (Christine) Rossi, is born.

1940   (June) The Rossi family, Maria and Emilio, son
Enrico (Rico), daughters Louise and Cristina, now
lives in Leith Walk above Shrubhill Café.
Mussolini declares war on Britain and France which
results in anti-Italian riots in Edinburgh and Glasgow.
Churchill implements a 'Collar the Lot' policy.
Emilio Rossi, imprisoned as an enemy alien. Italian
nationals who have not been interned, mainly
women, issued with relocation notices ordering them
to remove themselves twenty miles inland within
seventy-two hours. Maria Rossi taken to Kelso in the
Scottish Borders.

1940   (July) Sinking of the *Arandora Star*, a cruise ship
converted for the transportation of prisoners of war
to Canada. Emilio Rossi drowned along with 500
other Italians.

1943   (April) Marriage of Cristina Rossi and Alec Argent.

1944   (May) The Allies' victory: Battle of Montecassino.

1949   (August) Anne Argent (Anne Pia) is born.

1954   (September) Anne aged five, commences school at St
Margaret's Convent, Edinburgh.
Cristina, husband Alec and daughter Anne live

with Maria Rossi in Falcon Avenue, Morningside, Edinburgh.

1955   (August) Alec Argent, leaves.

1956   (May) Maria Rossi buys The Copper Kettle café in Bruntsfield Place and she, Cristina and Anne aged seven, move to a flat in Bruntsfield Terrace, Edinburgh.

1957   (September) Ernestina Coletta, an eighteen-year-old cousin, arrives from Viticuso.

1964   (May) Death of Maria Rossi.
Anne, aged fourteen, becomes a full-time boarder at St Margaret's Convent.

1966   (June) Alec and Cristina divorce.

October 1967 – June 1971 Anne awarded a Joint Honours degree, in Italian and French by the University of Edinburgh.

September 1969 – June 1970
Anne spends a year in France.

1970   (June – September) Anne attends the Universitá per Stranieri, Florence.

1971   (June – September) Anne works and studies in Florence.

1972   (June) Anne awarded Dip.Ed and PGCE. First teaching post at Notre Dame High School, Glasgow.

1974   (February) Anne moves back to Edinburgh.
Appointed Principal Teacher Guidance at St

Thomas of Aquin's High School, Edinburgh;
promoted to Assistant Headteacher, 1985.

1977   (July) Marriage to Paul Pia.

1980   (September) Birth of Camilla Francis Pia.

1985   (July) Birth of Roberta Anne Pia.

1988   (April) Birth of Sophie-Louise Pia.

1993   (January) Death of Cristina Rossi.

1995   (June) Anne is appointed as a Director of Glenrothes College.

1998   (April) Anne is appointed HM Inspector of Education. In 2000 Anne is seconded to the Ministerial Task Force for Adult Literacy and Numeracy in Scotland.

2007   (June) Anne's first visit to Holy Isle, a Buddhist-owned island off the coast of Arran.

2008   (November) At age fifty-nine, Anne is awarded a Doctorate of Education (Ed.D) by the University of Edinburgh .

2010   (November) Anne's visit to Plum Village, a community of Buddhists near Bordeaux, where she experiences her first encounter with Thay Nhat Hahn.

2012   (August) Anne takes Buddhist vows on Holy Isle.

Luath Press Limited

committed to publishing well written books worth reading

LUATH PRESS takes its name from Robert Burns, whose little collie Luath (*Gael.*, swift or nimble) tripped up Jean Armour at a wedding and gave him the chance to speak to the woman who was to be his wife and the abiding love of his life. Burns called one of the 'Twa Dogs' Luath after Cuchullin's hunting dog in Ossian's *Fingal.*
Luath Press was established in 1981 in the heart of Burns country, and is now based a few steps up the road from Burns' first lodgings on Edinburgh's Royal Mile. Luath offers you distinctive writing with a hint of unexpected pleasures.
Most bookshops in the UK, the US, Canada, Australia, New Zealand and parts of Europe, either carry our books in stock or can order them for you. To order direct from us, please send a £sterling cheque, postal order, international money order or your credit card details (number, address of cardholder and expiry date) to us at the address below. Please add post and packing as follows: UK – £1.00 per delivery address; overseas surface mail – £2.50 per delivery address; overseas airmail – £3.50 for the first book to each delivery address, plus £1.00 for each additional book by airmail to the same address. If your order is a gift, we will happily enclose your card or message at no extra charge.

Luath Press Limited
543/2 Castlehill
The Royal Mile
Edinburgh EH1 2ND
Scotland
Telephone: +44 (0)131 225 4326 (24 hours)
email: sales@luath. co.uk
Website: www. luath.co.uk